THOUGHT VIBRATION WORKBOOK

THOUGHT VIBRATION WORKBOOK

A Guide to Developing the Willpower to Attract Whatever You Desire

Based on the works of William Walker Atkinson

NOVELLA WILLIAMS

MARLEX
International Inc.

MARLEX INTERNATIONAL INC.
MIAMI FL

THOUGHT VIBRATION WORKBOOK

Based on the works of William Walker Atkinson

By Novella Williams

Copyright © 2013 Novella Williams

ISBN-13: 978-0991385508

ISBN-10: 0991385500

Cover design by Novella Williams. Page layout and formatting by Emily Beech.

DEDICATION

I dedicate this first book to my son, Quanti. You were in the background of my thoughts as I completed this book. Thank you my darling, for always being there for me, always supporting me even when it doesn't look like it. I just want you to know that I know that you love me. You, Nekita and Tiara have been and *will always be* the source of love and inspiration for me and the cause of my perpetual curiosity of life.

PREFACE

I was introduced to the phrase "cause and effect" when I began chanting NAM MYOHO RENGE KYO over 30 years ago. At that time I was angry at the world with every reason. I thank God for finding Nichiren's Buddhism. (Yes, you read that right!) In Buddhism it's said that as soon as you make a cause you get the effect. It may not manifest immediately but it inevitably will. Said another way, what goes around, comes around.

I have been engaged in the practice of using the power of words for even longer than that. I think that I got it from the Bible... just don't ask me when or where. I used to read that big black book on occasion as a youngster. Not by choice, but by default. Being an avid reader as a child, my mother discovered taking away my books was a very successful source of punishment when necessary. Since the only book left available to me was the Bible, I read it.

The greatest value derived from my experience of reading the Bible was my relationship to cause and effect. What you reap is what you sow. I also figured out that there was power in words. "Ask and it shall be given you". Even without the proper word definition, I knew I had the ability to "create". Initially, I thought it was something that everyone did. Although I didn't have a word for it, I instinctively knew what I was doing. I would want to do a thing, go somewhere or I'd suddenly have an idea about something. Little bits and pieces of information would pop into my head and if I followed them whatever I wanted got worked out.

I attended the Landmark Forum in 1992 in Detroit Michigan and life as I knew it was forever altered. My perception of life was transformed. My Buddhist teachings became clear. I finally registered that only I was responsible for my life. My chanting developed more power and focus because of my clarity. I used my Buddhist teachings and training along with the tools I was learning at Landmark to move to Florida and change my entire life.

After attending the Communications Course: Access to Power at Landmark I discovered that the "thing' that I did was called something. "The Power to Create". With this new found access I knew I could now tell others about this power. This is when I began to consciously create.

Somewhere along the way I also discovered I have a unique ability to take complicated things and break them down into bite sized pieces thus simplifying them. Not realizing it was a gift, it had went unnoticed and unappreciated by myself as well as others.

When I found The Science of Getting Rich by Wallace D. Wattles, it was such an expression of my life it became my little bible. As far as I was concerned, it could have been renamed to "The Secret of Getting Whatever You Want" because that's how I used it. I began to discover many other like-minded books from earlier decades and I dubbed their authors, "The Masters".

Because I love sharing what I learn, especially if it has the potential to enhance lives, I created classes and trainings for others who wanted to study and learn these age old lessons. Through training and coaching others I began to see the value of my unique gift of simplification. I designed exercises that "un-complicated" the material so it could help people to understand and practice the Law of Attraction in their everyday lives.

I firmly believe that there will be a tipping point where enough people will get the power of their words and together we will fill the world with love and acceptance, because we say so.

So without further ado my partner in completing this book, Emily Beech and I, as God's divine vessels, deliver this substance with energy and invincible determination. Thank you for patiently giving me your ear. I have completely enjoyed elaborating on these lessons; I hope you enjoy the practices as much as I did creating them!

CONTENTS

ACKNOWLEDGMENTS

I want to thank my dad, *Eddie Lee Warren*, for building my confidence by always assuring me that I could do anything, and my mother, *Mary Lou Warren*, for my strength, resilience and entrepreneurial spirit. A special thanks goes out to: Grandma *Darlene Ryor* who uncovered my love of organization, bringing order to my thoughts as well as my life. You could never even begin to know the difference you have made in the lives of so many because of this. *John and Susie Millonig* for being the epitome of generosity, kindness and compassion. My soul wants to be like yours when it grows up. *Henry Hardy* and *Jim Schauerte* for being my eternal playmates. *Gregg Hartmann* for his powerful listening of me. *Chata Dickson* for giving me the profound experience of unconditional love. A loving thank you to *Michael, Kendall, Sean London and Dominic* for causing me to become someone I don't know myself to be. Grand-mama loves you.

A very special thank you to *Emily Beech*, my prosperity partner. I am very clear that without you this workbook could not have happened. As God's divine vessels, Emily and I deliver this substance with energy and invincible determination. Thank you for patiently giving me your ear. I have completely enjoyed elaborating on these lessons, I hope you enjoy them too!

A loving thank you to all my spiritual sistas, in particular, Lee-Anne P., Debbie S., Karen W., Alexandra R., Otilia P. and Lisa R. You make such a profound difference in my life. This one's for you!

INTRODUCTION

Thought Vibration or the Law of Attraction in the Thought World was written by William Walker Atkinson in the early 1900's. This book breaks down in scientific terms of its time, the essential ingredients of thought vibrations and the mechanics of how it attracts. It explains on an elementary level how the law of vibration works. While there have been many upgrades to this conversation over the years the basic concept is clear and unadulterated.

How to get the most out of this book:
Thought Vibration was written in old English and may be difficult to understand at times. I was tempted to divide some of William's run-on sentences but (for the most part) I resisted the urge. Read it as if you are talking to someone. Actually, "scolding" would be more accurate. I suggest reading one chapter a week and doing the exercise. Then let it all sink in before going on to the next chapter. Take the time to contemplate his message and how it could make a difference in your life.

Each week comments will be posted from participants who have been using the workbook at MyProspserityAdviser.com. Just look for Thought Vibrations Workbook and see what others are saying about their experience. These exercises were designed to put each chapter into your life on an experiential level.

In closing let's forgive William Atkinson for any statements he makes in his manuscript that contradict current popular beliefs. We have made significant strides in understanding these powerful mechanisms we share as humans and yet we have much, much more understanding to go. Have fun and let us know how this book impacts your life.

CHAPTER ONE

The Law of Attraction in the Thought World

THE UNIVERSE is governed by Law - one great Law. Its manifestations are multiform, but viewed from the Ultimate there is but one Law. We are familiar with some of its manifestations, but are almost totally ignorant of certain others. Still we are learning a little more every day - the veil is being gradually lifted.

We speak learnedly of the Law of Gravitation, but ignore that equally wonderful manifestation, THE LAW OF ATTRACTION IN THE THOUGHT WORLD. We are familiar with that wonderful manifestation of Law which draws and holds together the atoms of which matter is composed. We recognize the power of the law that attracts bodies to the earth, that holds the circling worlds in their places, but we close our eyes to the mighty law that draws to us the things we desire or fear, that makes or mars our lives.

When we come to see that Thought is a force - a manifestation of energy - having a magnet-like power of attraction, we will begin to understand the why and wherefore of many things that have heretofore seemed dark to us. There is no study that will so well repay the student for his time and trouble as the study of the workings of this mighty law of the world of Thought - the Law of Attraction.

1

When we think we send out vibrations of a fine ethereal substance, which are as real as the vibrations manifesting light, heat, electricity, magnetism. That these vibrations are not evident to our five senses is no proof that they do not exist. A powerful magnet will send out vibrations and exert a force sufficient to attract to itself a piece of steel weighing a hundred pounds, but we can neither see, taste, smell, hear nor feel the mighty force. These thought vibrations, likewise, cannot be seen, tasted, smelled, heard nor felt in the ordinary way; although it is true there are on record cases of persons peculiarly sensitive to psychic impressions who have perceived powerful thought-waves, and very many of us can testify that we have distinctly felt the thought vibrations of others, both whilst in the presence of the sender and at a distance.

Telepathy and its kindred phenomena are not idle dreams. Light and heat are manifested by vibrations of a far lower intensity than those of Thought, but the difference is solely in the rate of vibration. The annals of science throw an interesting light upon this question. Prof. Elisha Gray, an eminent scientist, says in his little book, "The Miracles of Nature":

"There is much food for speculation in the thought that there exist sound-waves that no human ear can hear, and color-waves of light that no eye can see. The long, dark, soundless space between 40,000 and 400,000,000,000,000 vibrations per second, and the infinity of range beyond 700,000,000,000,000 vibrations per second, where light ceases, in the universe of motion, makes it possible to indulge in speculation."

M. M. Williams, in his work entitled "Short Chapters in Science," says:

"There is no gradation between the most rapid undulations or trembling's that produce our sensation of sound, and the slowest of those which give rise to our sensations of gentlest warmth. There is a huge gap between them, wide enough to include another world of motion, all lying between our world of sound and our world of heat and light; and there is no good reason whatever for supposing

that matter is incapable of such intermediate activity, or that such activity may not give rise to intermediate sensations, provided there are organs for taking up and sensitizing their movements."

I cite the above authorities merely to give you food for thought, not to attempt to demonstrate to you the fact that thought vibrations exist. The last-named fact has been fully established to the satisfaction of numerous investigators of the subject, and a little reflection will show you that it coincides with your own experiences.

We often hear repeated the well-known Mental Science statement, "Thoughts are Things," and we say these words over without consciously realizing just what is the meaning of the statement. If we fully comprehended the truth of the statement and the natural consequences of the truth back of it, we should understand many things which have appeared dark to us, and would be able to use the wonderful power, Thought Force, just as we use any other manifestation of Energy.

As I have said, when we think we set into motion vibrations of a very high degree, but just as real as the vibrations of light, heat, sound, electricity. And when we understand the laws governing the production and transmission of these vibrations we will be able to use them in our daily life, just as we do the better known forms of energy. That we cannot see, hear, weigh or measure these vibrations is no proof that they do not exist.

There exist waves of sound which no human ear can hear, although some of these are undoubtedly registered by the ear of some of the insects, and others are caught by delicate scientific instruments invented by man; yet there is a great gap between the sounds registered by the most delicate instrument and the limit which man's mind, reasoning by analogy, knows to be the boundary line between sound waves and some other forms of vibration. And there are light waves which the eye of man does not register, some of which may be detected by more delicate instruments, and many more so fine that the instrument has not yet been invented which will detect them, although improvements are being made every year and the unexplored field gradually lessened.

As new instruments are invented, new vibrations are registered by them - and yet the vibrations were just as real before the invention of the instrument as afterward. Supposing that we had no instruments to register magnetism - one might be justified in denying the existence of that mighty force, because it could not be tasted, felt, smelt, heard, seen, weighted or measured. And yet the mighty magnet would still send out waves of force sufficient to draw to it pieces of steel weighing hundreds of pounds.

Each form of vibration requires its own form of instrument for registration. At present the human brain seems to be the only instrument capable of registering thought waves, although occultists say that in this century scientists will invent apparatus sufficiently delicate to catch and register such impressions. And from present indications it looks as if the invention named might be expected at any time. The demand exists and undoubtedly will be soon supplied. But to those who have experimented along the lines of practical telepathy no further proof is required than the results of their own experiments.

We are sending out thoughts of greater or less intensity all the time, and we are reaping the results of such thoughts. Not only do our thought waves influence ourselves and others, but they have a drawing power - they attract to us the thoughts of others, things, circumstances, people, "luck," in accord with the character of the thought uppermost in our minds. Thoughts of Love will attract to us the Love of others; circumstances and surroundings in accord with the thought; people who are of like thought. Thoughts of Anger, Hate, Envy, Malice and Jealousy will draw to us the foul brood of kindred thoughts emanating from the minds of others;

circumstances in which we will be called upon to manifest these vile thoughts and will receive them in turn from others; people who will manifest disharmony; and so on.

A strong thought or a thought long continued, will make us the center of attraction for the corresponding thought waves of others. Like attracts like in the Thought World - as ye sow so shall ye reap. Birds of a feather flock together in the Thought World - curses like chickens come home to roost, and bringing their friends with them. The man or woman who is filled with Love sees Love on all sides and attracts the Love of others. The man with hate in his heart gets all the Hate he can stand. The man who thinks Fight generally runs up against all the Fight he wants before he gets through. And so it goes, each gets what he calls for over the wireless telegraphy of the Mind. The man who rises in the morning feeling "grumpy" usually manages to have the whole family in the same mood before the breakfast is over. The "nagging" woman generally finds enough to gratify her "nagging" propensity during the day.

This matter of Thought Attraction is a serious one. When you stop to think of it you will see that a man really makes his own surroundings, although he blames others for it. I have known people who understood this law to hold a positive, calm thought and be absolutely unaffected by the disharmony surrounding them. They were like the vessel from which the oil had been poured on the troubled waters - they rested safely and calmly whilst the tempest raged around them. One is not at the mercy of the fitful storms of Thought after he has learned the workings of the Law.

We have passed through the age of physical force on to the age of intellectual supremacy, and are now entering a new and almost unknown field, that of psychic power. This field has its established laws and we should acquaint ourselves with them or we will be crowded to the wall as are the ignorant on the planes of effort. I will endeavor to make plain to you the great underlying principles of this new field of energy which is opening up before us, that you may be able to make use of this great power and apply it for legitimate and worthy purposes, just as men are using steam, electricity and other forms of energy today.

CHAPTER 1 SUMMARY - The Law of Attraction in the Thought World

Thought is energy and it attracts other thoughts of like nature, much like the pull of gravity or a magnet attracting metal objects. Like a magnet or gravity, one cannot touch, taste, see, hear or feel it yet it exists.

Key Points:

- Thought is a form of vibrational energy that attracts like objects. A magnet attracts metal; Thought vibrations attract similar thoughts.
- The vibrational pull of thoughts happen unseen by the human eye much like the magnet.
- The distinction of thoughts pulling similar things to it is called the Law of Attraction.
- You are attracting like thoughts to you all the time whether you are aware of it or not.
- Your surroundings are things you have pulled to you by your thoughts: i.e. THOUGHT ATTRACTION.

EXERCISE 1

1. Make a list of the major areas of your life. (I.e. relationship, finances, education, romance, career, family, health, job, spirituality, etc.) Pick one area of your life that you would like to prosper. Use a journal or the lines below.

2. Write down 10 to a 100 things that you can think of that you say to yourself or others about this area. The Good. The Bad. The Ugly. For this exercise to work you must be brutally honest with yourself and tell it like it is.

I highly recommend you to do this right now before proceeding any further.

(Example: Area: Relationship | 1. I can never meet the right guy.)

AREA OF LIFE _____

1.

2.

3.

4.

5.

6.

7.

8.

9.

10.

CHAPTER TWO

Thought Waves and their Process of Reproduction

LIKE a stone thrown into the water, thought produces ripples and waves which spread out over the great ocean of thought. There is this difference, however: the waves on the water move only on a level plane in all directions, whereas thought waves move in all directions from a common center, just as do the rays from the sun.

Just as we here on earth are surrounded by a great sea of air, so are we surrounded by a great sea of Mind. Our thought waves move through this vast mental ether, extending, however, in all directions, as I have explained, becoming somewhat lessened in intensity according to the distance traversed, because of the friction occasioned by the waves coming in contact with the great body of Mind surrounding us on all sides.

These thought waves have other qualities differing from the waves on the water. They have the property of reproducing themselves; in this respect they resemble sound waves rather than waves upon the water. Just as a note of the violin will cause the thin glass to vibrate and "sing," so will a strong thought tend to awaken similar vibrations in minds attuned to receive it.

Many of the "stray thoughts" which come to us are but reflections or answering vibrations to some strong thought sent out by another. But unless our minds are attuned to receive it, the thought will not likely affect us. If we are thinking high and great thoughts, our minds acquire a certain keynote corresponding to the character of the thoughts we have been thinking. And, this keynote once established, we will be apt to catch the vibrations of other minds keyed to the same thought.

On the other hand, let us get into the habit of thinking thoughts of an opposite character, and we will soon be echoing the low order of thought emanating from the minds of the thousands thinking along the same lines. We are largely what we have thought ourselves into being, the balance being represented by the character of the suggestions and thought of others, which have reached us either directly by verbal suggestions or telepathically by means of such thought waves.

Our general mental attitude, however, determines the character of the thought waves received from others as well as the thoughts emanating from ourselves. We receive only such thoughts as are in harmony with the general mental attitude held by ourselves; the thoughts not in harmony affecting us very little, as they awaken no response in us.

The man who believes thoroughly in himself and maintains a positive strong mental attitude of Confidence and Determination is not likely to be affected by the adverse and negative thoughts of Discouragement and Failure emanating from the minds of other persons in whom these last qualities predominate.

At the same time these negative thoughts, if they reach one whose mental attitude is pitched on a low key, deepen his negative state and add fuel to the fire which is consuming his strength, or, if you prefer this figure, serve to further smother the fire of his energy and activity. We attract to us the thoughts of others of the same order of thought.

The man who thinks success will be apt to get into tune with the minds of others thinking likewise, and they will help him, and he them. The man who allows his mind to dwell constantly upon thoughts of failure brings himself into close touch with the minds of other "failure" people, and each will tend to pull the other down still more.

The man who thinks that all is evil is apt to see much evil, and will be brought into contact with others who will seem to prove his theory. And the man who looks for good in everything and everybody will be likely to attract to himself the things and people corresponding to his thought. We generally see that for which we look.

You will be able to carry this idea more clearly if you will think of the Marconi wireless instruments, which receive the vibrations only from the sending instrument which has been attuned to the same key, while other telegrams are passing through the air in near vicinity without affecting the instrument. The same law applies to the operations of thought. We receive only that which corresponds to our mental attunement.

If we have been discouraged, we may rest assured that we have dropped into a negative key, and have been affected not only by our own thoughts but have also received the added depressing thoughts of similar character which are constantly being sent out from the minds of other unfortunates who have not yet learned the law of attraction in the thought world.

And if we occasionally rise to heights of enthusiasm and energy, how quickly we feel the inflow of the courageous, daring, energetic, positive thoughts being sent out by the live men and women of the world. We recognize this without much trouble when we come in personal contact with people and feel their vibrations, depressing or invigorating, as the case may be.

But the same law operates when we are not in their presence, although less strongly. The mind has many degrees of pitch, ranging from the highest positive note to the lowest negative note, with many notes in between, varying in pitch according to their respective distance from the positive or negative extreme.

When your mind is operating along positive lines you feel strong, buoyant, bright, cheerful, happy, confident and courageous, and are enabled to do your work well, to carry out your intentions, and progress on your roads to Success. You send out strong positive thought, which affects others and causes them to co-operate with you or to follow your lead, according to their own mental keynote.

When you are playing on the extreme negative end of the mental keyboard you feel depressed, week, passive, dull, fearful, cowardly. And you find yourself unable to make progress or to succeed. And your effect upon others is practically nil. You are led by, rather than leading others, and are used as a human doormat or football by more positive persons.

In some persons the positive element seems to predominate, and in others the negative quality seems to be more in evidence. There are, of course, widely varying degrees of positive-ness and negative-ness, and B may be negative to A, while positive to C. When two people first meet there is generally a silent mental conflict in which their respective minds test their quality of positive-ness, and fix their relative position toward each other.

This process may be unconscious in many cases, but it occurs nevertheless. The adjustment is often automatic, but occasionally the struggle is so sharp - the opponents being so well matched - that the matter forces itself into the consciousness of the two people. Sometimes both parties are so much alike in their degrees of positive-ness that they fail to come to terms, mentally; they never really are able to get along with each other, and they are either mutually repelled and separate or else stay together amid constant broils and wrangling.

We are positive or negative to everyone with whom we have relations. We may be positive to our children, our employees and dependents, but we are at the same time negative to others to whom we occupy inferior positions, or whom we have allowed to assert themselves over us. Of course, something may occur and we will suddenly become more positive than the man or woman to whom we have heretofore been negative. We frequently see cases of this kind.

And as the knowledge of these mental laws becomes more general we will see many more instances of persons asserting themselves and making use of their new found power. But remember you possess the power to raise the keynote of your mind to a positive pitch by an effort of the will. And, of course, it is equally true that you may allow yourself to drop into a low, negative note by carelessness or a weak will.

There are more people on the negative plane of thought than on the positive plane, and consequently there are more negative thought vibrations in operation in our mental atmosphere. But, happily for us, this is counterbalanced by the fact that a positive thought is infinitely more powerful than a negative one, and if by force of will we raise ourselves to a higher mental key we can shut out the depressing thoughts and may take up the vibrations corresponding with our changed mental attitude. This is one of the secrets of the affirmations and autosuggestions used by the several schools of Mental Science and other New Thought cults.

There is no particular merit in affirmations of themselves, but they serve a twofold purpose: (1) They tend to establish new mental attitudes within us and act wonderfully in the direction of character- building - the science of making ourselves over. (2) They tend to raise the mental keynote so that we may get the benefit of the positive thought waves of others on the same plane of thought. Whether or not we believe in them, we are constantly making affirmations.

The man who asserts that he can and will do a thing - and asserts it earnestly - develops in himself the qualities conducive to the well doing of that thing, and at the same time places his mind in the proper key to receive all the thought waves likely to help him in the doing.

If, on the other hand, one says and feels that he is going to fail, he will choke and smother the thoughts coming from his own subconscious mentality which are intended to help him, and at the same time will place himself in tune with the Failure-Thought of the world - and there is plenty of the latter kind of thought around, I can tell you.

Do not allow yourselves to be affected by the adverse and negative thoughts of those around you. Rise to the upper chambers of your mental dwelling, and key yourself up to a strong pitch, away above the vibrations on the lower planes of thought. Then you will not only be immune to their negative vibrations but will be in touch with the great body of strong positive thought coming from those of your own plane of development.

My aim will be to direct and train you in the proper use of thought and will, that you may have yourself well in hand and may be able to strike the positive key at any moment you may feel it necessary. It is not necessary to strike the extreme note on all occasions.

The better plan is to keep yourself in a comfortable key, without much strain, and to have the means at command whereby you can raise the pitch at once when occasion demands. By this knowledge you will not be at the mercy of the old automatic action of the mind, but may have it well under your own control.

Development of the will is very much like the development of a muscle - a matter of practice and gradual improvement. At first it is apt to be tiresome, but at each trial one grows stronger until the new strength becomes real and permanent.

Many of us have made ourselves positive under sudden calls or emergencies. We are in the habit of "bracing up" when occasion demands. But by intelligent practice you will be so much strengthened that your habitual state will be equal to your "bracing up" stage now, and then when you find it necessary to apply the spur you will be able to reach a stage not dreamed of at present.

 Do not understand me as advocating a high tension continuously. This is not at all desirable, not only because it is apt to be too much of a strain upon you but also because you will find it desirable to relieve the tension at times and become receptive that you may absorb impressions. It is well to be able to relax and assume a certain degree of receptiveness, knowing that you are always able to spring back to the more positive state at will.

The habitually strongly positive man loses much enjoyment and recreation. Positive, you give out expressions; receptive, you take in impressions. Positive, you are a teacher; receptive, a pupil. It is not only a good thing to be a good teacher, but it is also very important to be a good listener at times.

CHAPTER 2 SUMMARY - Thought Waves and their Process of Reproduction

Thoughts reproduce themselves. Your strong thoughts are picked up by those around you with similar thoughts and are reflected back to you. You are attuned to receive those thoughts similar to your own mental attitude. The type of thought energy sent out is also what you draw in whether it be the thought of failure or success.

Key Points:

- Thought vibrations have the property of reproducing themselves.
- Your strong thoughts are picked up by those around you with similar thoughts.
- You are attuned to receive only thoughts similar to your mental attitude.
- Positive thought energy attracts positive thoughts and negative energy attracts negative thoughts.
- Positive thought energy repels negative thoughts and negative energy repels positive thoughts.
- This happens whether one knows it or not whether one believes it or not.

EXERCISE 2

Go back to the list that you made for LESSON 1.

1. Notice that some of the things on your list are positive, some are negative. These are your energy thoughts.

2. For each of the negative energy thoughts, circle the number at the beginning.

3. When you are finished, total your negative energy thoughts and your positive energy thoughts.

Using the space below, see if you can re-frame the Negative Energy Thought statements so that they reflect Positive Energy Thoughts.

_____ Number of Positive Energy Thoughts

_____ Number of Negative Energy Thoughts (Reframed these into positive statements)

(Example: I can never meet the right guy - Re-frame: The right guy is out there and we will find each other soon)

Negative Energy Thought::

Re-frame:

CHAPTER THREE

A Talk about the Mind

MAN has but one mind, but he has many mental faculties, each faculty being capable of functioning along two different lines of mental effort. There are no distinct dividing lines separating the two several functions of a faculty, but they shade into each other as do the colors of the spectrum.

An Active effort of any faculty of the mind is the result of a direct impulse imparted at the time of the effort. A Passive effort of any faculty of the mind is the result of either a preceding Active effort of the same mind; an Active effort of another along the lines of suggestion;

Thought Vibrations from the mind of another; Thought impulses from an ancestor, transmitted by the laws of heredity (including impulses transmitted from generation to generation from the time of the original vibratory impulse imparted by the Primal Cause - which impulses gradually unfold, and unsheathe, when the proper state of evolutionary development is reached).

The Active effort is new-born - fresh from the mint, whilst the Passive effort is of less recent creation, and, in fact, is often the result of vibratory impulses imparted in ages long past. The Active effort makes its own way, brushing aside the impeding vines and kicking from its path the obstructing stones. The Passive effort travels along the beaten path.

A thought-impulse, or motion-impulse, originally caused by an Active effort of faculty, may become by continued repetition, or habit, strictly automatic, the impulse given it by the repeated Active effort developing a strong momentum, which carries it on, along Passive lines, until stopped by another Active effort or its direction changed by the same cause.

On the other hand, thought-impulses, or motion-impulses, continued along Passive lines may be terminated or corrected by an Active effort. The Active function creates, changes or destroys. The Passive function carries on the work given it by the Active function and obeys orders and suggestions.

The Active function produces the thought-habit, or motion-habit, and imparts to it the vibrations, which carry it on along the Passive lines thereafter. The Active function also has the power to send forth vibrations which neutralize the momentum of the thought-habit, or motion-habit; it also is able to launch a new thought-habit, or motion-habit, with stronger vibrations, which overcomes and absorbs the first thought, or motion, and substitutes the new one.

All thought-impulses, or motion-impulses, once started on their errands, continue to vibrate along passive lines until corrected or terminated by subsequent impulses imparted by the Active function, or other controlling power. The continuance of the original impulse adds momentum and force to it, and renders its correction or termination more difficult. This explains that which is called "the force of habit."

I think that this will be readily understood by those who have struggled to overcome a habit which had been easily acquired. The Law applies to good habits as well as bad. The moral is obvious.

Several of the faculties of the mind often combine to produce a single manifestation. A task to be performed may call for the combined exercise of several faculties, some of which may manifest by Active effort and others by Passive effort.

The meeting of new conditions - new problems - calls for the exercise of Active effort; whilst a familiar problem, or task, can be easily handled by the Passive effort without the assistance of his more enterprising brother.

There is in Nature an instinctive tendency of living organisms to perform certain actions, the tendency of an organized body to seek that which satisfies the wants of its organism. This tendency is sometimes called Appetency. It is really a Passive mental impulse, originating with the impetus imparted by the Primal Cause, and transmitted along the lines of evolutionary development, gaining strength and power as it progresses.

The impulse of the Primal Cause is assisted by the powerful upward attraction exerted by THE ABSOLUTE. In plant life this tendency is plainly discernible, ranging from the lesser exhibitions in the lower types to the greater in the higher types. It is that which is generally spoken of as the "life-force" in plants. It is, however, a manifestation of rudimentary mentation, functioning along the lines of Passive effort.

In some of the higher forms of plant life there appears a faint color of independent "life action" - a faint indication of choice of volition. Writers on plant life relate many remarkable instances of this phenomenon. It is, undoubtedly, an exhibition of rudimentary Active mentation.

In the lower animal kingdom a very high degree of Passive mental effort is found. And, varying in degree in the several families and species, a considerable amount of Active mentation is apparent. The lower animal undoubtedly possesses Reason only in a lesser degree than man, and, in fact, the display of volitional mentation exhibited by an intelligent animal is often nearly as high as that shown by the lower types of man or by a young child.

As a child, before birth, shows in its body the stages of the physical evolution of man, so does a child, before and after birth - until maturity - manifest the stages of the mental evolution of man.

Man, the highest type of life yet produced, at least upon this planet, shows the highest form of Passive mentation, and also a much higher development of Active mentation than is seen in the lower animals, and yet the degrees of that power vary widely among different men.

The different degrees of Active mentation are plainly noticeable; these degrees not depending by any means upon the amount of "culture," social position or educational advantages possessed by the individual: Mental Culture and Mental Development are two very different things. You have but to look around you to see the different stages of the development of Active mentation in man.

 The reasoning of many men is scarcely more than Passive mentation, exhibiting but little of the qualities of volitional thought. They prefer to let other men think for them. Active mentation tires them and they find the instinctive, automatic, Passive mental process much easier. Their minds work along the lines of least resistance. They are but little more than human sheep.

Among the lower animals and the lower types of men, Active mentation is largely confined to the grosser faculties - the more material plane; the higher mental faculties working along the instinctive, automatic lines of the Passive function. As the lower forms of life progressed in the evolutionary scale, they developed new faculties which were latent within them. These faculties always manifested in the form of rudimentary Passive functioning, and afterwards worked up through higher Passive forms, until the Active functions were brought into play.

The evolutionary process still continues, the invariable tendency being toward the goal of highly developed Active mentation. This evolutionary progress is caused by the vibratory impulse imparted by the Primal Cause, aided by the uplifting attraction of THE ABSOLUTE. This law of evolution is still in progress, and man is beginning to develop new powers of mind, which, of course, are first manifesting themselves along the lines of Passive effort.

Some men have developed these new faculties to a considerable degree, and it is possible that before long Man will be able to exercise them along the line of their Active functions. In fact, this power has already been attained by a few. This is the secret of the Oriental occultists, and of some of their Occidental brethren.

The amenability of the mind to the will can be increased by properly directed practice. That which we are in the habit of referring to as the "strengthening of the Will" is in reality the training of the mind to recognize and absorb the Power Within. The Will is strong enough, it does not need strengthening, but the mind needs to be trained to receive and act upon the suggestions of the Will.

The Will is the outward manifestation of the I AM. The Will current is flowing in full strength along the spiritual wires; but you must learn how to raise the trolley-pole to touch it before the mental car will move. This is a somewhat different idea from that which you have been in the habit of receiving from writers on the subject of Will Power, but it is correct, as you will demonstrate to your own satisfaction if you will follow up the subject by experiments along the proper lines.

The attraction of THE ABSOLUTE is drawing man upward, and the vibratory force of the Primal Impulse has not yet exhausted itself. The time of evolutionary development has come when man can help himself. The man who understands the Law can accomplish wonders by means of the development of the powers of the mind; whilst the man who turns his back upon the truth will suffer from his lack of knowledge of the Law.

He who understands the laws of his mental being, develops his latent powers and uses them intelligently. He does not despise his Passive mental functions, but makes good use of them also, charges them with the duties for which they are best fitted, and is able to obtain wonderful results from their work, having mastered them and trained them to do the bidding of the Higher Self.

When they fail to do their work properly he regulates them, and his knowledge prevents him from meddling with them unintelligently, and thereby doing himself harm. He develops the faculties and powers latent within him and learns how to manifest them along the line of Active mentation as well as Passive. He knows that the real man within him is the master to whom both Active and Passive functions are but tools. He has banished Fear, and enjoys Freedom. He has found himself. He has learned the secret of the I AM.

CHAPTER 3 SUMMARY - A Talk about the Mind

The mind travels along 2 different lines of mental effort, active and passive. There is no distinct dividing lines and they tend to blend into each other. Active effort produces thought and motion habits. Active effort is right now, forging new paths, giving orders and making suggestions. New conditions and new problems are handled by active effort. Only active effort can change or stop passive effort. Familiar problems and tasks are handled by passive effort. Passive effort impulses are generated from past ancestry, heredity, past generations and basic instincts. It travels the beaten path, is repetitive and obeys orders and suggestions. Passive effort continues along its path and left undisturbed will cause a habit or way of being extremely difficult to be changed or stopped without exerting a great deal of active effort.

Key points:

- The mind functions along two different lines of mental lines of effort. Active and Passive.
- Active and Passive, while different do not always show up separately.
- Your thoughts are generated along both Active and Passive lines.
- The Active thoughts are new born, fresh from the mint. (i.e. new creations)
- The Passive thoughts result from past thought energy, thought vibrations from others or heredity.
- Active thoughts create new conditions and opportunities for new habits to form.
- Areas of life that are working well by Passive thoughts should not be disturbed or regulated.
- Use Active thoughts to change any unwanted habits by using I AM.

EXERCISE 3

1. What is your "I AM" in life? What do you say about yourself?

2. Write down the first thought you had when reading the areas below. Be very honest with yourself. Trying to make yourself look good here will not get the results you want.

(Example: RELATIOSHIPS, I AM: Scared to death to get married)

RELATIONSHIPS, I AM:

FAMILY, I AM:

MONEY, I AM:

MY CAREER, I AM:

MY HEALTH, I AM: SP

IRITUALITY, I AM:

EDUCATION, I AM:

ROMANCE, I AM:

CREATIVITY, I AM:

TIME MANAGEMENT, I AM:

ORGANIZATION, I AM:

OUTLOOK ON LIFE, I AM:

CHAPTER FOUR

Mind Building

MAN can build up his mind and make it what he wills. In fact, we are mind-building every hour of our lives, either consciously or unconsciously. The majority of us are doing the work unconsciously, but those who have seen a little below the surface of things have taken the matter in hand and have become conscious creators of their own mentality.

They are no longer subject to the suggestions and influences of others but have become masters of themselves. They assert the "I," and compel obedience from the subordinate mental faculties. The "I" is the sovereign of the mind, and what we call WILL is the instrument of the "I."

Of course, there is something in back of this, and the Universal Will is higher than the Will of the Individual, but the latter is in much closer touch with the Universal Will than is generally supposed. When one conquers the lower self, and asserts the "I," he becomes in close touch with the Universal Will and partakes largely of its wonderful power.

The moment one asserts the "I," and "finds himself," he establishes a close connection between the Individual Will and the Universal Will. But before he is able to avail himself of the mighty power at his command, he must first effect the Mastery of the lower self.

Think of the absurdity of Man claiming to manifest powers, when he is the slave of the lower parts of his mental being, which should be subordinate. Think of a man being the slave of his moods, passions, animal appetites and lower faculties, and at the same time trying to claim the benefits of the Will. Now, I am not preaching asceticism, which seems to me to be a confession of weakness. I am speaking of Self-Mastery - the assertion of the "I" over the subordinate parts of oneself.

In the higher view of the subject, this "I" is the only real Self, and the rest is the non-self; but our space does not permit the discussion of this point, and we will use the word "self" as meaning the entire man. Before a man can assert the "I" in its full strength he must obtain the complete mastery of the subordinate parts of the self. All things are good when we learn to master them, but no "thing" is good when it masters us.

Just so long as we allow the lower portions of the self to give us orders, we are slaves. It is only when the "I" mounts his throne and lifts the scepter, that order is established and things assume their proper relation to each other. We are finding no fault with those who are swayed by their lower selves - they are in a lower grade of evolution, and will work up in time. But we are calling the attention of those who are ready, to the fact that the Sovereign must assert his will, and that the subjects must obey.

Orders must be given and carried out. Rebellion must be put down, and the rightful authority insisted upon. And the time to do it is Now. You have been allowing your rebellious subjects to keep the King from his throne. You have been allowing the mental kingdom to be misgoverned by irresponsible faculties. You have been the slaves of Appetite, Unworthy Thoughts, Passion and Negative-ness.

The Will has been set aside and Low Desire has usurped the throne. It is time to re-establish order in the mental kingdom. You are able to assert the mastery over any emotion, appetite, passion or class of thoughts by the assertion of the Will. You can order Fear to go to the rear; Jealousy to leave your presence; Hate to depart from your sight; Anger to hide itself; Worry to cease troubling you; Uncontrolled Appetite and Passion to bow in submission and to become humble slaves instead of masters - all by the assertion of the "I."

You may surround yourself with the glorious company of Courage, Love and Self-Control, by the same means. You may put down the rebellion and secure peace and order in your mental kingdom if you will but utter the mandate and insist upon its execution.

Before you march forth to empire, you must establish the proper internal condition - must show your ability to govern you own kingdom. The first battle is the conquest of the lesser self by the Real Self.

AFFIRMATION

I AM Asserting the Mastery of My Real Self

Repeat these words earnestly and positively during the day at least once an hour, and particularly when you are confronted with conditions which tempt you to act on the lines of the lesser self instead of following the course dictated by the Real Self. In the moment of doubt and hesitation say these words earnestly, and your way will be made clear to you. Repeat them several times after you retire and settle yourself to sleep. But be sure to back up the words with the thought inspiring them, and do not merely repeat them parrot-like.

Form the mental image of the Real Self asserting its mastery over the lower planes of your mind - see the King on his Throne. You will become conscious of an influx of new thought, and things which have seemed hard for you will suddenly become much easier. You will feel that you have yourself well in hand, and that YOU are the master and not the slave. The thought you are holding will manifest itself in action, and you will steadily grow to become that which you have in mind.

EXERCISE

Fix the mind firmly on the higher Self and draw inspiration from it when you feel led to yield to the promptings of the lower part of your nature. When you are tempted to burst into Anger - assert the "I," and your voice will drop. Anger is unworthy of the developed Self. When you feel vexed and cross, remember what you are, and rise above your feeling. When you feel Fearful, remember that the Real Self fears nothing, and assert Courage. When you feel Jealousy inciting, think of your higher nature, and laugh. And so on, asserting the Real Self and not allowing the things on the lower plane of mentality to disturb you. They are unworthy of you, and must be taught to keep their places. Do not allow these things to master you - they should be your subjects, not your masters. You must get away from this plane, and the only way to do so is to cut loose from these phases of thought which have been "running things" to suit themselves. You may have trouble at the start, but keep at it and you will have that satisfaction which comes only from conquering the lower parts of our nature. You have been a slave long enough - now is the time to free yourselves. If you will follow these exercises faithfully you will be a different being by the end of the year, and will look back with a pitying smile to your former condition. But it takes work. This is not child's play but a task for earnest men and women, Will YOU make the effort?

CHAPTER 4 SUMMARY - Mind Building

Whether you are aware of it or not you are "mind building" constantly. Most people are unconsciously building their minds or "creating". Some people have become masters at this and are no longer subject to the suggestions and opinions of others. You can build your mind and make it what you will. You do this by asserting the "I". The lower parts of your mental being are your moods, passions, uncontrolled appetites, emotions, jealousy, fear, anger, hate and worry. Some people have become slaves to their lower parts. The way to reestablish mastery over your lower parts when they show up, declare often, "I am asserting the mastery of my real self".

Key Points:

- Subordinate mental factors are the lower selves. (i.e., moods, passions, animal appetites, jealousy and negativity)
- "Will" is an instrument of the "I".
- Without asserting the "I am", man is slave to his lower selves.
- The first battle is to conquer the lower selves by the real self.
- When you assert mastery over your lower selves, you conquer fear.
- Reestablish mastery over your lower parts with the affirmation: I AM ASSERTING THE MASTERY OF MY REAL SELF.
- You can build your mind by asserting the "I am".

APPLYING SPECIAL ATTENTION: Every morning upon rising and every evening before bed say the following affirmation: I AM ASSERTING THE MASTERY OF MY REAL SELF.

EXERCISE 4

To free yourself from the slavery of the lower thoughts that have been "running things" to suit themselves:

1. Notice the YOU that notices the lower parts and fix your attention there. Be inspired that YOU are not those parts.

2. Begin to create yourself newly, fill in the blanks below and say each out loud.

3. Go through your list of I AM's and choose the ones that are important to you and shift your thought vibrations.

(Example: I AM a completely capable new mother)

I AM ASSERTING THE MASTERY OF MY REAL SELF.

I AM:

I AM ASSERTING THE MASTERY OF MY REAL SELF.

I AM:

I AM ASSERTING THE MASTERY OF MY REAL SELF.

I AM:

I AM ASSERTING THE MASTERY OF MY REAL SELF.

I AM:

CHAPTER FIVE

The Secret of the Will

WHILE psychologists may differ in their theories regarding the nature of the Will, none deny its existence, nor question its power. All persons recognize the power of strong Will - all see how it may be used to overcome the greatest obstacles. But few realize that the Will may be developed and strengthened by intelligent practice. They feel that they could accomplish wonders if they had a strong Will, but instead of attempting to develop it, they content themselves with vain regrets. They sigh, but do nothing.

Those who have investigated the subject closely know that Will Power, with all its latent possibilities and mighty powers, may be developed, disciplined, controlled and directed, just as may be any other of Nature's forces. It does not matter what theory you may entertain about the nature of the Will, you will obtain the results if you practice intelligently.

Personally, I have a somewhat odd theory about the Will. I believe that every man has, potentially, a strong Will, and that all he has to do is to train his mind to make use of it. I think that in the higher regions of the mind of every man is a great store of Will Power awaiting his use. The Will current is running along the psychic wires, and all that it is necessary to do is to raise the mental trolley-pole and bring down the power for your use.

And the supply is unlimited, for your little storage battery is connected with the great powerhouse of the Universal Will Power, and the power is inexhaustible. Your Will does not need training - but your Mind does. The mind is the instrument and the supply of Will Power is proportionate to the fineness of the instrument through which it manifests. But you needn't accept this theory if you don't like it. This lesson will fit your theory as well as mine.

He who has developed his mind so that it will allow the Will Power to manifest through it, has opened up wonderful possibilities for himself. Not only has he found a great power at his command, but he is able to bring into play, and use, faculties, talents and abilities of whose existence he has not dreamed. This secret of the Will is the magic key which opens all doors.

The late Donald G. Mitchell once wrote: "Resolve is what makes a man manifest; not puny resolve, but crude determination; not errant purpose - but that strong and indefatigable will which treads down difficulties and danger, as a boy treads down the heaving frost-lands of winter; which kindles his eye and brain with a proud pulse-beat toward the unattainable. Will makes men giants."

Many of us feel that if we would but exert our Will, we might accomplish wonders. But somehow we do not seem to want to take the trouble - at any rate; we do not get to the actual willing point. We put it off from time to time, and talk vaguely of "some day," but that "some day" never comes.

We instinctively feel the power of the Will, but we haven't enough energy to exercise it, and so drift along with the tide, unless perhaps some friendly difficulty arises, some helpful obstacle appears in our path, or some kindly pain stirs us into action, in either of which cases we are compelled to assert our Will and thus begin to accomplish something.

The trouble with us is that we do not want to do the thing enough to make us exert our Will Power. We don't want to hard enough. We are mentally lazy and of weak Desire. If you do not like the word Desire substitute for it the word "Aspiration." (Some people call the lower impulses Desires, and the higher, Aspirations - it's all a matter of words, take you choice.) That is the trouble.

Let a man be in danger of losing his life – Let a woman be in danger of losing a great love - and you will witness a startling exhibition of Will Power from an unexpected source. Let a woman's child be threatened with danger, and she will manifest a degree of Courage and Will that sweeps all before it. And yet the same woman will quail before a domineering husband, and will lack the Will to perform a simple task. A boy will do all sorts of work if he but considers it play, and yet he can scarcely force himself to cut a little firewood.

Strong Will follows strong Desire. If you really want to do a thing very much, you can usually develop the Will Power to accomplish it. The trouble is that you have not really wanted to do these things, and yet you blame your Will. You say that you do want to do it, but if you stop to think you will see that you really want to do something else more than the thing in question. You are not willing to pay the price of attainment. Stop a moment and analyze this statement and apply it in your own case. You are mentally lazy - that's the trouble.

Don't talk to me about not having enough Will. You have a great storehouse of Will awaiting your use, but you are too lazy to use it. Now, if you are really in earnest about this matter, get to work and first find out what you really want to do - then start to work and do it. Never mind about the Will Power - you'll find a full supply of that whenever you need it. The thing to do is to get to the point where you will resolve to do. That the real test - the resolving.

Think of these things a little, and make up your mind whether or not you really want to be a "Willer" sufficiently hard to get to work. Many excellent essays and books have been written on this subject, all of which agree regarding the greatness of Will Power, the most enthusiastic terms being used; but few have anything to say about how this power may be acquired by those who have it not, or who possess it in but a limited degree.

Some have given exercises designed to "strengthen" the Will, which exercises really strengthen the Mind so that it is able to draw upon its store of power. But they have generally overlooked the fact that in autosuggestion is to be found the secret of the development of the mind so that it may become the efficient instrument of the Will.

AUTOSUGGESTION

I AM Using My Will Power

Say these words several times earnestly and positively, immediately after finishing this article. Then repeat them frequently during the day, at least once an hour, and particularly when you meet something that calls for the exercise of Will Power. Also repeat them several times after you retire and settle yourself for sleep. Now, there is nothing in the words unless you back them up with the thought. In fact, the thought is "the whole thing," and the words only pegs upon which to hang the thought. So think of what you are saying, and mean what you say. You must use Faith at the start, and use the words with a confident expectation of the result. Hold the steady thought that you are drawing on your storehouse of Will Power, and before long you will find that thought is taking form in action, and that your Will Power is manifesting itself. You will feel an influx of strength with each repetition of the words. You will find yourself overcoming difficulties and bad habits, and will be surprised at how things are being smoothed out for you.

EXERCISE

Perform at least one disagreeable task each day during the month. If there is any especially disagreeable task which you would like to shirk, that is the one for you to perform. This is not given to you in order to make you self-sacrificing or meek, or anything of that sort - it is given you to exercise your Will. Anyone can do a pleasant thing cheerfully, but it takes Will to do the unpleasant thing cheerfully; and that is how you must do the work. It will prove a most valuable discipline to you. Try it for a month and you will see where "it comes in." If you shirk this exercise you had better stop right here and acknowledge that you do not want Will Power, and are content to stay where you are and remain a weakling.

CHAPTER 5 SUMMARY - The Secret of the Will

The Will may be developed and strengthened by intelligent practice. First you must train your mind to make use of it. Many people feel they could accomplish wonders if they could but exert their will. The truth is that we are mentally lazy and have weak desire. We don't "want to" badly enough. You must use Faith at the start, and use the words with a confident expectation of the result. Hold the steady thought that you are drawing on your storehouse of Will Power and affirm, "I am using my will power".

Key Points:

- The Will can be developed and strengthened by intelligent practice.
- Everyone has a strong Will if you can TRAIN your mind to use it.
- Most people are mentally lazy with weak desires and will not act on their desires until absolutely forced.
- Find out what you really want to do, then get to work and do it.
- Affirmations are the secret for strengthening the mind, creating strong Will Power.

EXERCISE 5

If you are not doing the exercises in this book you may as well stop wasting your time now! Just acknowledge that you have no Will Power and are content to stay where you are. If not, then…

1. Make a list of things in your life where you lack Will power to do a thing. You must be brutally honest with yourself.

2. Cheerfully do one thing every day that you don't want to do.

3. Try saying loudly, "I AM using my will power" when you first wake up, when you retire and throughout the day.

Create a structure to remind yourself to do this every day for 21 days. (i.e. put it on your calendar, post it on the refrigerator, put it in your car, etc.)

Examples: LIST: Saving Money, cleaning my house, planning…

I am using my will power to clean my house.

I am using my will power to make more money.

CHAPTER SIX

How to Become Immune to Injurious Thought Attraction

THE first thing to do is to begin to "cut out" Fear and Worry. Fear-thought is the cause of much unhappiness and many failures. You have been told this thing over and over again, but it will bear repeating. Fear is a habit of mind which has been fastened upon us by negative race-thought, but from which we may free ourselves by individual effort and perseverance.

Strong expectancy is a powerful magnet. He of the strong, confident desire attracts to him the things best calculated to aid him - persons, things circumstances, surroundings; if he desires them hopefully, trustfully, confidently, calmly. And, equally true, he who Fears a thing generally manages to start into operation forces which will cause the thing he feared to come upon him.

Don't you see, the man who Fears really expects the feared thing, and the eyes of the Law is the same as if he really had wished for or desired it? The Law is operative in both cases - the principle is the same.

The best way to overcome the habit of Fear is to assume the mental attitude of Courage, just as the best way to get rid of darkness is to let in the light. It is a waste of time to fight a negative thought-habit by recognizing its force and trying to deny it out of existence by mighty efforts.

The best, surest, easiest and quickest method is to assume the existence of the positive thought desired in its place; and by constantly dwelling upon the positive thought, manifest it into objective reality. Therefore, instead of repeating, "I'm not afraid," say boldly, "I am full of Courage," "I am Courageousness."

You must assert, "There's nothing to fear," which, although in the nature of a denial, simply denies the reality of the object causing fear rather than admitting the fear itself and then denying it. To overcome fear, one should hold firmly to the mental attitude of Courage. He should think Courage, say Courage, act Courage.

He should keep the mental picture of Courage before him all the time, until it becomes his normal mental attitude. Hold the ideal firmly before you and you will gradually grow to its attainment - the ideal will become manifest. Let the word "Courage" sink deeply into your mind, and then hold it firmly there until the mind fastens it in place.

Think of yourself as being Courageous - see yourself as acting with Courage in trying situations. Realize that there is nothing to Fear - that Worry and Fear never helped anyone, and never will. Realize that Fear paralyzes effort, and that Courage promotes activity. The confident, fearless, expectant, "I Can and I Will" man is a mighty magnet. He attracts to himself just what is needed for his success. Things seem to come his way, and people say he is "lucky." Nonsense! "Luck" has nothing to do with it. It's all in the Mental Attitude.

The Mental Attitude of the "I Can't" or the "I'm Afraid" man determines his measure of success. There's no mystery whatsoever about it. You have but to look about you to realize the truth of what I have said. Did you ever know a successful man who did not have the "I Can and I will" thought strong within him? Why, he will walk all around the "I Can't" man, who has perhaps even more ability.

The first mental attitude brought to the surface latent qualities, as well as attracted help from outside; whilst the second mental attitude not only attracted "I Can't" people and things, but also kept the man's own powers from manifesting themselves.

I have demonstrated the correctness of these views, and so have many others, and the number of people who know these things is growing every day. Don't waste your Thought-Force, but use it to advantage. Stop attracting to yourself failure, unhappiness, disharmony, sorrow - begin now and send out a current of bright, positive, happy thought. Let your prevailing thought be "I Can and I Will;" think "I Can and I Will;" dream "I Can and I Will;" say "I Can and I Will;" and act "I Can and I Will". Live on the "I Can and I Will" plane, and before you are aware of it, you will feel the new vibrations manifesting themselves in action; will see them bring results; will be conscious of the new point of view; will realize that your own is coming to you.

You will feel better, act better, see better, BE better in every way, after you join the "I Can and I Will" brigade. Fear is the parent of Worry, Hate, Jealousy, Malice, Anger, Discontent, Failure and all the rest. The man who rids himself of Fear will find that the rest of the brood has disappeared. The only way to be Free is to get rid of Fear. Tear it out by the roots.

I regard the conquest of Fear as the first important step to be taken by those who wish to master the application of Thought Force. So long as Fear masters you, you are in no condition to make progress in the realm of Thought, and I must insist that you start to work at once to get rid of this obstruction.

You CAN do it - if you only go about it in earnest. And when you have ridded yourself of the vile thing, life will seem entirely different to you - you will feel happier, freer, stronger, more positive, and will be more successful in every undertaking of Life.

Start it today, make up your mind that this intruder must GO - do not compromise matters with him, but insist upon an absolute surrender on his part. You will find the task difficult at first, but each time you oppose him he will grow weaker, and you will be stronger. Shut off his nourishment - starve him to death - he cannot live in a thought atmosphere of Fearlessness.

So, start to fill your mind with good, strong, Fearless thoughts - keep yourself busy thinking Fearlessness, and Fear will die of his own accord. Fearlessness is positive - Fear is negative, and you may be sure that the positive will prevail. So long as Fear is around with his "but," "if," "suppose," "I'm afraid," "I can't," "what if," and all the rest of his cowardly suggestions, you will not be able to use your Thought Force to the best advantage. Once get him out of the way, you will have clear sailing, and every inch of thought-sail will catch the wind. He is a Jonah. Overboard with him! (The whale that swallows him will have my sympathy.)

I advise that you start in to do some of the things which you feel you could do if you were not afraid to try. Start to work to do these things, affirming Courage all the way through, and you will be surprised to see how the changed mental attitude will clear away obstacles from your path, and will make things very much easier than you had anticipated. Exercises of this kind will develop you wonderfully, and you will be much gratified at the result of a little practice along these lines.

There are many things before you awaiting accomplishment, which you can master if you will only throw aside the yoke of Fear - if you will only refuse to accept the race suggestion, and will boldly assert the "I" and its power. And the best way to vanquish Fear is to assert "Courage" and stop thinking of Fear.

By this plan you will train the mind into new habits of thought, thus eradicating the old negative thoughts which have been pulling you down, and holding you back. Take the word "Courage" with you as your watchword and manifest it in action. Remember, the only thing to fear is Fear, and - well, don't even fear "Fear", for he's a cowardly chap at the best, who will run if you show a brave front.

CHAPTER 6 SUMMARY - How to Become Immune to Injurious Thought Attraction

That which you fear, you powerfully draw toward you though expectation. To overcome fear, you need to hold on to the mental attitude of Courage. Fear is the parent of Worry, Hate, Jealousy, Malice, Anger, Discontent, Failure and all the rest. The only way to be Free is to get rid of Fear. Tear it out by the roots - make up your mind that this intruder must GO! Shut off his nourishment. The best way to vanquish Fear is to assert "Courage" and stop thinking of Fear. Develop Courage to overcome Fear. Courage is not the absence of fear. It is strength in the presence of fear. Fill your mind with good, strong, fearless thoughts.

Key points:

- Fear thought is the cause of much unhappiness and many failures. Fear is a habit which you can overcome by adding courage.
- Strong expectancy is a powerful magnet.
- Confidence attracts confidence and fear attracts the thing feared.
- Never say "I am afraid". Use the words, "I am courageous and there is nothing to fear".
- Fear paralyzes effort and courage promotes activity.
- Using but, if, suppose, I'm afraid, I can't, and what if, will not allow you to use your thought force at maximum advantage.
- Let your prevailing thoughts be "I Can and I Will;" think "I Can and I Will;" dream "I Can and I Will;" say "I Can and I Will;" and act "I Can and I Will." Live on the "I Can and I Will" plane.

EXERCISE 6

To take the damaging thoughts out of your head:

1. Create a list of at least 5 things you would do if you were not afraid. Do not speak in generalities. Be specific. (Look at your previous lists for suggestions.)
2. Commit to doing one thing that you can do in a day and schedule it on your calendar.
3. Allow the words "I can and I will have Courage" to sink deeply into your mind, then hold it firmly there until the mind fastens it in place.
4. Think of yourself as being Courageous – imagine yourself acting with Courage in a difficult situation.

State what you would do (NOT what you would not do) if you were courageous. Example: If I were not afraid, I would ask my boss for a raise.

If I were not afraid, I would:

If I were not afraid, I would:

If I were not afraid, I would:

If I were not afraid, I would:

If I were not afraid, I would:

CHAPTER SEVEN

The Transmutation of Negative Thought

WORRY is the child of Fear - if you kill out Fear, Worry will die for want of nourishment. This advice is very old, and yet it is always worthy of repetition, for it is a lesson of which we are greatly in need. Some people think that if we kill out Fear and Worry we will never be able to accomplish anything.

I have read editorials in the great journals in which the writers held that without Worry one can never accomplish any of the great tasks of life, because Worry is necessary to stimulate interest and work. This is nonsense, no matter who utters it. Worry never helped one to accomplish anything; on the contrary, it stands in the way of accomplishment and attainment.

The motive underlying action and "doing things" is Desire and Interest. If one earnestly desires a thing, he naturally becomes very much interested in its accomplishment, and is quick to seize upon anything likely to help him to gain the thing he wants. More than that, his mind starts up a work on the subconscious plane that brings into the field of consciousness many ideas of value and importance.

Desire and Interest are the causes that result in success. Worry is not Desire. It is true that if one's surroundings and environments become intolerable, he is driven in desperation to some efforts

49

that will result in throwing off the undesirable conditions and in the acquiring of those more in harmony with his desire.

But this is only another form of Desire - the man desires something different from what he has; and when his desire becomes strong enough his entire interest is given to the task, he makes a mighty effort, and the change is accomplished. But it wasn't Worry that caused the effort. Worry could content itself with wringing its hands and moaning, "Woe is me," and wearing its nerves to a frazzle, and accomplishing nothing.

Desire acts differently. It grows stronger as the man's conditions become intolerable, and finally when he feels the hurt so strongly that he can't stand it any longer, he says, "I won't stand this any longer - l will make a change," and lo! Then Desire springs into action. The man keeps on "wanting" a change the worst way (which is the best way) and his Interest and Attention being given to the task of deliverance, he begins to make things move.

Worry never accomplished anything. Worry is negative and death producing. Desire and Ambition are positive and life producing. A man may worry himself to death and yet nothing will be accomplished, but let that man transmute his worry and discontent into Desire and Interest, coupled with a belief that he is able to make the change - the "I Can and I Will" idea - then something happens.

Yes, Fear and Worry must go before we can do much. One must proceed to cast out these negative intruders, and replace them with Confidence and Hope. Transmute Worry into keen Desire. Then you will find that Interest is awakened, and you will begin to think things of interest to you.

Thoughts will come to you from the great reserve stock in your mind and you will start to manifest them in action. Moreover you will be placing yourself in harmony with similar thoughts of others, and will draw to you aid and assistance from the great volume of thought waves with which the world is filled.

One draws to himself thought waves corresponding in character with the nature of the prevailing thoughts in his one mind - his mental attitude. Then again he begins to set into motion the great Law of Attraction, whereby he draws to him others likely to help him, and is, in turn, attracted to others who can aid him.

This Law of Attraction is no joke, no metaphysical absurdity, but is a great live working principle of Nature, as anyone may learn by experimenting and observing. To succeed in anything you must want it very much - Desire must be in evidence in order to attract.

The man of weak desires attracts very little to himself. The stronger the Desire the greater the force set into motion. You must want a thing hard enough before you can get it. You must want it more than you do the things around you, and you must be prepared to pay the price for it. The price is the throwing overboard of certain lesser desires that stand in the way of the accomplishment of the greater one.

Comfort, ease, leisure, amusements, and many other things may have to go (not always, though). It all depends on what you want. As a rule, the greater the thing desired, the greater the price to be paid for it. Nature believes in adequate compensation. But if you really Desire a thing in earnest, you will pay the price without question; for the Desire will dwarf the importance of the other things.

You say that you want a thing very much, and are doing everything possible toward its attainment? Pshaw! You are only playing Desire. Do you want the thing as much as a prisoner wants freedom - as much as a dying man wants life? Look at the almost miraculous things accomplished by prisoners desiring freedom. Look how they work through steel plates and stonewalls with a bit of stone. Is your desire as strong as that? Do you work for the desired thing as if your life depended upon it? Nonsense! You don't know what Desire is.

I tell you if a man wants a thing as much as the prisoner wants freedom, or as much as a strongly vital man wants life, then that man will be able to sweep away obstacles and impediments apparently immovable. The key to attainment is Desire, Confidence, and Will. This key will open many doors. Fear paralyzes Desire - it scares the life out of it. You must get rid of Fear.

There have been times in my life when Fear would get hold of me and take a good, firm grip on my vitals, and I would lose all hope; all interest; all ambition; all desire. But, thank the Lord, I have always managed to throw off the grip of the monster and face my difficulty like a man; and lo! Things would seem to be straightened out for me somehow.

Either the difficulty would melt away or I would be given means to overcome, or get around, or under or over it. It is strange how this works. No matter how great is the difficulty, when we finally face it with courage and confidence in ourselves, we seem to pull through somehow, and then we begin to wonder what we were scared about.

This is not a mere fancy, it is the working of a mighty law, which we do not as yet fully understand, but which we may prove at any time. People often ask: "It's all very well for you New Thought people to say 'Don't worry,' but what's a person to do when he thinks of all the possible things ahead of him, which might upset him and his plans?" Well, all that I can say is that the man is foolish to bother about thinking of troubles to come at some time in the future.

The majority of things that we worry about don't come to pass at all; a large proportion of the others come in a milder form than we had anticipated, and there are always other things which come at the same time which help us to overcome the trouble.

The future holds in store for us not only difficulties to be overcome, but also agents to help us in overcoming the difficulties. Things adjust themselves. We are prepared for any trouble which may come upon us, and when the time comes we somehow find ourselves able to meet it.

God not only tempers the wind to the shorn lamb, but He also tempers the shorn lamb to the wind. The winds and the shearing do not come together; there is usually enough time for the lamb to get seasoned, and then he generally grows new wool before the cold blast comes. It has been well said that nine-tenths of the worries are over things which never comes to pass, and that the other tenth is over things of little or no account. So what's the use in using up all your reserve force in fretting over future troubles, if this be so? Better wait until your troubles really come before you worry.

You will find that by this storing up of energy you will be able to meet about any sort of trouble that comes your way. What is it that uses up all the energy in the average man or woman, anyway? Is it the real overcoming of difficulties, or the worrying about impending troubles? It's always "Tomorrow, tomorrow," and yet tomorrow never comes just as we feared it would. Tomorrow is alright; it carries in its grip good things as well as troubles.

Bless my soul, when I sit down and think over the things which I once feared might possibly descend upon me, I laugh! Where are those feared things now? I don't know — have almost forgotten that I ever feared them. You do not need fight Worry - that isn't the way to overcome the habit. Just practice concentration, and then learn to concentrate upon something right before you, and you will find that the worry thought has vanished.

The mind can think of but one thing at a time, and if you concentrate upon a bright thing, the other thing will fade away. There are better ways of overcoming objectionable thoughts than by fighting them. Learn to concentrate upon thoughts of an opposite character, and you will have solved the problem. When the mind is full of worry thoughts, it cannot find time to work out plans to benefit you. But when you have concentrated upon bright, helpful thoughts, you will discover that it will start to work subconsciously; and when the time comes you will find all sorts of plans and methods by which you will be able to meet the demands upon you.

Keep your mental attitude right, and all things will be added unto you. There's no sense in worrying; nothing has ever been gained by it, and nothing ever will be. Bright, cheerful and happy thoughts attract bright, cheerful and happy things to us - worry drives them away. Cultivate the right mental attitude.

CHAPTER 7 SUMMARY - Transmutation of Negative Thought

As a rule, the greater the thing desired, the greater the price to be paid for it. Nature believes in adequate compensation. The key to attainment is Desire, Confidence, and Will. This key will open many doors. Once Interest is awakened, you will begin to think of things that interest you. Thoughts will come to you from the great reserve stock in your mind and you will start to manifest them in action. Fear and worry stand in the way of Desire and Interest and takes all of its energy. The mind can think of only one thing at a time. Being Present in the Moment is an excellent practice for asserting the Will; it soothes the mind and takes away fear and worry. Fighting worry is not the way to overcome fear.

Key Points:

- Worry is the child of Fear –when you remove Fear, worry will leave as well.
- Worry stands in the way of Desire and Interest.
- Worry takes all the energy from Desire and Interest.
- Once Interest is awakened, you will begin to think of things of interest to you.
- Thoughts will come to you from the great reserve stock in your mind and you will start to manifest them in action.
- The mind can think of only one thing at a time.
- Your "Will" can choose what your mind thinks about.
- Being Present in the Moment is an excellent practice for asserting the Will over the negative thoughts of the mind.
- Fear and worry come from the past experiences of the mind.
- Being in the "present moment" takes away fear and worry and soothes the mind.

EXERCISE 7

Exercises to get you present in the moment:

- Sit in a quiet position. Move your tongue around in your mouth. Notice that less than 5 seconds ago you didn't notice it at all. Notice how it feels, how it is moving, notice whatever you are noticing about the tongue in your mouth.

- Your "third eye" is a spot in the center of your forehead. With your eyes open, notice this spot in the center of your forehead. Imagine that you are looking at. Feel it with your mind. Focus on it and keep it present as long as you can.

- Rub your index finger with your thumb. Feel the sensation of your thumb rubbing your index finger. Now try to reverse it and notice the sensation of your index finger rubbing on your thumb.

- Without reaching up to touch it, identify the very top of your head. It may take a few minutes but you will begin to feel the very center of your skull. Continue this experience as long as you can.

CHAPTER EIGHT

The Law of Mental Control

YOUR thoughts are either faithful servants or tyrannical masters - just as you allow them to be. You have the say about it; take your choice. They will either go about your work under direction of the firm will, doing it the best they know how, not only in your waking hours, but when you are asleep - some of our best mental work being performed for us when our conscious mentality is at rest, as is evidenced by the fact that when the morning comes we find troublesome problems have been worked out for us during the night, after we had dismissed them from our minds - apparently; or they will ride all over us and make us their slaves if we are foolish enough to allow them to do so.

More than half the people of the world are slaves of every vagrant thought which may see fit to torment them. Your mind is given you for your good and for your own use - not to use you. There are very few people who seem to realize this and who understand the art of managing the mind. The key to the mystery is Concentration. A little practice will develop within every man the power to use the mental machine properly.

When you have some mental work to do concentrate upon it to the exclusion of everything else, and you will find that the mind will get right down to business - to the work at hand - and matters will be cleared up in no time. There is an absence of friction, and all waste motion or lost power is obviated. Every pound of energy is put to use, and every revolution of the mental driving wheel counts for something. It pays to be able to be a competent mental engineer. And the man who understands how to run his mental engine knows that one of the important things is to be able to stop it when the work has been done.

He does not keep putting coal in the furnace, and maintaining a high pressure after the work is finished, or when the day's portion of the work has been done, and the fires should be banked until the next day. Some people act as if the engine should be kept running whether there was any work to be done or not, and then they complain if it gets worn out and wobbles and needs repairing.

These mental engines are fine machines, and need intelligent care. To those who are acquainted with the laws of mental control it seems absurd for one to lie awake at night fretting about the problems of the day, or more often, of the morrow. It is just as easy to slow down the mind as it is to slow down an engine, and thousands of people are learning to do this in these days of New Thought.

The best way to do it is to think of something else - as far different from the obtruding thought as possible. There is no use fighting an objectionable thought with the purpose of "downing" it - that is a great waste of energy, and the more you keep on saying, "I won't think of this thing!" the more it keeps on coming into your mind, for you are holding it there for the purpose of hitting it.

Let it go; don't give it another thought; fix the mind on something entirely different, and keep the attention there by an effort of the will. A little practice will do much for you in this direction. There is only room for one thing at a time in the focus of attention; so put all your attention upon one thought, and the others will sneak off. Try it for yourself.

CHAPTER 8 SUMMARY - The Law of Mental Control

There is no use fighting an objectionable thought with the purpose of keeping it down. The fight will only strengthen it and give it power. You must fix your mind on something entirely different, and keep the attention there by an effort of will. A little practice will do much for you in this direction. There is only room for one thing at a time in the focus of attention; so put all your attention upon one thought, and the others will fall away.

Key Points:

- Some of your best mental work occurs when you are asleep.
- Your mind is for your good use, not to use you.
- The practice of concentration can develop a man's mental power.
- It's useless to try and resist something you "don't want to think" by suppressing it.
- Your resistance to an undesirable thought will only strengthen it and give it power.
- You can slow the mind by thinking something differently.
- Instead of resisting, practice using will power.
- You can only hold one thought in your mind at a time, so put all your attention upon one thought, and the others will fall away.

EXERCISE 8

1. Make a list of 5 objectionable worries/thoughts. (Get suggestions from your lists from Exercise 5 & 6.)

2. Re-frame each to be a positive I CAN statement.

Example: Worry – I don't have enough money. Re-frame – I don't have any money at the moment but I can and will make some soon.

Worry/fear:

Positive Re-frame:

Worry/fear:

Positive Re-frame:

Worry/fear:

Positive Re-frame:

Worry/fear:

Positive Re-frame:

Worry/fear:

Positive Re-frame:

CHAPTER NINE

Asserting the Life Force

I have spoken to you of the advantage of getting rid of Fear. Now I wish to put LIFE into you. Many of you have been going along as if you were dead - no ambition – no energy - no vitality - no interest - no life. This will never do. You are stagnating. Wake up and display a few signs of life! This is not the place in which you can stalk around like a living corpse - this is the place for wide-awake, active, live people, and a good general awakening is what is needed; although it would take nothing less than a blast from Gabriel's trumpet to awaken some of the people who are stalking around thinking that they are alive, but who are really dead to all that makes life worthwhile.

We must let Life flow through us, and allow it to express itself naturally. Do not let the little worries of life, or the big ones either, depress you and cause you to lose your vitality. Assert the Life Force within you, and manifest it in every thought, act and deed, and before long you will be exhilarated and fairly bubbling over with vitality and energy.

Put a little life into your work - into your pleasures - into yourself. Stop doing things in a half-headed way, and begin to take an interest in what you are doing, saying and thinking. It is astonishing how much interest we may find in the ordinary things

61

of life if we will only wake up. There are interesting things all around us - interesting events occurring every moment - but we will not be aware of them unless we assert our life force and begin to actually live instead of merely existing.

No man or woman ever amounted to anything unless he or she put life into the tasks of everyday life - the acts - the thoughts. What the world needs is live men and women. Just look into the eyes of the people whom you meet, and see how few of them are really alive. The most of them lack that expression of conscious life which distinguishes the man who lives from the one who simply exists.

I want you to acquire this sense of conscious life so that you may manifest it in your life and show what Mental Science has done for you. I want you to get to work today and begin to make yourselves over according to the latest pattern. You can do this if you will only take the proper interest in the task. AFFIRMATION AND EXERCISE Fix in your mind the thought that the "I" within you is very much alive and that you are manifesting life fully, mentally and physically. And keep this though there, aiding yourself with constant repetitions of the watchword.

Don't let the thought escape you, but keep pushing it back into the mind. Keep it before the mental vision as much as possible. Repeat the watchword when you awaken in the morning - say it when you retire at night. And say it at meal times, and whenever else you can during the day – at least once an hour. Form the mental picture of yourself as filled with Life and Energy. Live up to it as far as possible.

When you start in to perform a task say "I AM Alive" and mix up as much life as possible in the task. If you find yourself feeling depressed, say "I AM Alive," and then take a few deep breaths, and with each inhalation let the mind hold the thought that you are breathing in Strength and Life, and as you exhale, hold the thought that you are breathing out all the old, dead, negative conditions and are glad to get rid of them. Then finish up with an earnest, vigorous affirmation: "I AM Alive," and mean it when you say it too. And let your thoughts take form in action. Don't rest content with merely saying that you are alive, but prove it with your acts. Take an interest in doing things, and don't go around "mooning" or daydreaming. Get down to business, and LIVE.

CHAPTER 9 SUMMARY - Asserting the Life-Force

Wake up to your life and assert the Life Force within you by declaring loudly "I AM ALIVE". Manifest being alive in every thought, act and deed. Become exhilarated and fairly bubbling over with vitality and energy. Think before you speak, act or do something. Do it with enthusiasm. Form the mental picture of yourself as filled with Life and Energy. Say "I AM ALIVE" with as much life as possible. Look people in the eye and say, "Hi! What a wonderful day!" Notice the lack of interest in many people. Notice the lack of Life and Energy. If you are asked, "Why is it a wonderful day?" Say "I AM ALIVE!" Notice the vibrational pull, when you are in high spirits you can pull people up to that vibrational level.

Key Points:

- We must let Life flow through us, and allow it to express itself naturally.
- Manifest the life force in every thought, act and deed.
- Put a little life into your work - into your pleasures - into yourself.
- No man or woman ever amounted to anything unless he or she put life into the tasks of everyday life
- Discontinue doing things half-heartedly.
- The "I" within you is very much alive and that you are manifesting life fully, mentally and physically.
- If you find yourself feeling depressed, say "I AM Alive."
- Take an interest in doing things, and don't go around "mooning" or daydreaming. Get down to business, and LIVE.

EXERCISE 9

To pull yourself into an enlivened state:

Visualize yourself as filled with Life and Energy. Say "I AM ALIVE" at least once hourly.

Become exhilarated and fairly bubbling over with vitality and energy. Act ten times more excited than you do normally.

Look people in the eye and say, "Hi! What a wonderful day!

1. Do this for at least one week.
2. At the end of 7 days write in your journal the experience of your actions using the prompts below.

   a. How did this exercise make you feel? *(ex: I felt stupid, I felt exhilarated, it was interesting how people reacted etc.)*
   b. What did you notice about other people?
   c. What conclusions did you draw from this exercise?

.

CHAPTER TEN

Training the Habit Mind

PROFESSOR William James, the well-known teacher of, and writer upon Psychology very truly says:

"The great thing in all education is to make our nervous system our ally instead of our enemy. For this we must make automatic and habitual, as early as possible, as many useful actions as we can and as carefully guard against growing into ways that are likely to be disadvantageous.

In the acquisition of a new habit, or the leaving off of an old one we must take care to launch ourselves with as strong and decided initiative as possible. Never suffer an exception to occur until the new habit is securely rooted in your life. Seize the very first possible opportunity to act on every resolution you make and on every emotional prompting you may experience, in the direction of the habits you aspire to gain."

This advice is along the lines familiar to all students of Mental Science, but it states the matter more plainly than the majority of us have done. It impresses upon us the importance of passing on to the subconscious mind the proper impulses, so that they will become automatic and "second nature."

Our subconscious mentality is a great storehouse for all sorts of suggestions from ourselves and others and, as it is the "habit-mind," we must be careful to send it the proper material from which it may make habits. If we get into the habit of doing certain things, we may be sure that the subconscious mentality will make it easier for us to do just the same thing over and over again, easier each time, until finally we are firmly bound with the ropes and chains of the habit, and find it more or less difficult, sometimes almost impossible, to free ourselves from the hateful thing.

We should cultivate good habits against the hour of need. The time will come when we will be required to put forth our best efforts, and it rests with us today whether that hour of need shall find us doing the proper thing automatically and almost without thought, or struggling to do it bound down and hindered with the chains of things opposed to that which we desire at that moment.

We must be on guard at all times to prevent the forming of undesirable habits. There may be no special harm in doing a certain thing today, or perhaps again tomorrow, but there may be much harm in setting up the habit of doing that particular thing. If you are confronted with the question: "Which of these two things should I do?" the best answer is: "I will do that which I would like to become a habit with me."

In forming a new habit, or in breaking an old one, we should throw ourselves into the task with as much enthusiasm as possible, in order to gain the most ground before the energy expends itself when it meets with friction from the opposing habits already formed.

We should start in by making as strong an impression as possible upon the subconscious mentality. Then we should be constantly on guard against temptations to break the new resolution "just this once." This "just once" idea kills off more good resolutions than any other one cause. The moment you yield "just this once, you introduce the thin edge of the wedge that will, in the end, split your resolution into pieces.

Equally important is the fact that each time you resist temptation the stronger does your resolution become. Act upon your resolution as early and as often as possible, as with every manifestation of thought in action, the stronger does it become. You are adding to the strength of your original resolution every time you back it up with action.

The mind has been likened to a piece of paper that has been folded. Ever afterwards it has a tendency to fold in the same crease - unless we make a new crease or fold, when it will follow the last lines. And the creases are habits - every time we make one it is so much easier for the mind to fold along the same crease afterward. Let us make our mental creases in the right direction.

CHAPTER 10 SUMMARY - Training the Habit-Mind

We need to cultivate good habits against the hour of need. The time will come when we will be required to put forth our best efforts, and it rests with us today whether that hour of need shall find us doing the proper thing automatically and almost without thought, or struggling to do it bound and hindered with the chains of things opposed to that which we desire at that moment.

Key Points:

- We must practice good habits so that they are there when we need them most.
- When the time comes we must be prepared to do the proper thing automatically and almost without thought or struggle.
- If you are confronted with a choice, choose that which you would like to become a habit.
- Create a list of habits which you don't like and decide to conquer them.
- Begin to inquire into which habits you would like to change.

EXERCISE 10

Habits that you would like to change:

1. Make a list of habits you would like to change. Began with the list below and say what you dislike about that habit.

2. Write "I now do that which I want to become a habit with me and I can and I will..."

Example: Habit: often late; I say – I don't get enough sleep; new habit – I can and I will be on time for the next 21 days.

Habit _____

What I don't like about it _____

New habit "I CAN AND I WILL"

_____

Habit _____

What I don't like about it _____

New habit "I CAN AND I WILL"

_____

Habit _____

What I don't like about it _____

New habit "I CAN AND I WILL"

_____

CHAPTER ELEVEN

The Psychology of Emotion

One is apt to think of the emotions as independent from habit. We easily may think of one acquiring habits of action, and even of thinking, but we are apt to regard the emotions as something connected with "feeling" and quite divorced from intellectual effort.

Yet, notwithstanding the distinction between the two, both are dependent largely upon habit, and one may repress, increase, develop, and change one's emotions, just as one may regulate habits of action and lines of thought It is an axiom of psychology that "Emotions deepen by repetition."

If a person allows a state of feeling to thoroughly take possession of him, he will find it easier to yield to the same emotion the second time, and so on, until the particular emotion or feeling becomes second nature to him. If an undesirable emotion shows itself inclined to take up a permanent abode with you, you had better start to work to get rid of it, or at least to master it. And the best time to do this is at the start; for each repetition renders the habit more firmly entrenched, and the task of dislodging it more difficult.

Were you ever jealous? If so, you will remember how insidious was its first approach; how subtly it whispered hateful suggestions into your willing ear, and how gradually it followed up such suggestions, until, finally you began to see green. (Jealousy has an effect upon the bile, and causes it to poison the blood. This is why the idea of green is always associated with it.)

Then you will remember how the thing seemed to grow, taking possession of you until you scarcely could shake it off. You found it much easier to become jealous the next time. It seemed to bring before you all sorts of objects apparently justifying your suspicions and feeling. Everything began to look green – the green-eyed monster waxed fat. And so it is with every feeling or emotion.

If you give way to a fit of rage, you will find it easier to become angry the next time, on less provocation. The habit of feeling and acting "mean" does not take long to firmly settle itself in its new home if encouraged.

Worry is a great habit for growing and waxing fat. People start by worrying about big things, and then begin to worry and fret about some smaller thing. And then the merest trifle worries and distresses them.

They imagine that all sorts of evil things are about to befall them. If they start on a journey they are certain there is going to be a wreck. If a telegram comes, it is sure to contain some dreadful tidings. If a child seems a little quiet, the worrying mother is positive it is going to fall ill and die. If the husband seems thoughtful, as he revolves some business plan in his mind, then the good wife is convinced that he is beginning to cease to love her, and indulges in a crying spell.

And so it goes - worry, worry, worry - each indulgence making the habit more at home. After a while the continued thought shows itself in action. Not only is the mind poisoned by the blue thoughts, but the forehead shows deep lines between the eyebrows, and the voice takes on that whining, rasping tone so common among worry-burdened people. The condition of mind known as "fault-finding" is another emotion that grows fat with exercise.

First, fault is found with this thing, then with that, and finally with everything. The person becomes a chronic "nagger" - a burden to friends and relatives, and a thing to be avoided by outsiders. Women make the greatest naggers. Not because men are any better, but simply because a man nagger apt to have the habit knocked out of him by other men who will not stand his nonsense - he find that he is making things too hot for himself and he reforms; while a woman has more of a chance to indulge in the habit.

But this nagging is all a matter of habit. It grows from small beginnings, and each time it is indulged in it throws out another root, branch, or tendril, and fastens itself the closer to the one who has given it soil in which to grow. Envy, un-charitableness, gossip scandal-mongering, are all habits of this kind. The seeds are in every human breast, and only need good soil and a little watering to become lusty and strong.

Each time you give way to one of these negative emotions, the easier do you make it for a recurrence of the same thing, or similar ones. Sometimes by encouraging one unworthy emotion, you find that you have given room for the growth of a whole family of these mental weeds.

Now, this is not a good old orthodox preachment against the sin of bad thoughts. It is merely a calling of your attention to the law underlying the psychology of emotion. Nothing new about it - old as the hills - so old that many of us have forgotten all about it. If you wish to manifest these constantly disagreeable and unpleasant traits, and to suffer the unhappiness that comes from them, by all means do so - that is your own business, and privilege.

It's none of mine, and I am not preaching at you - it keeps me busy minding my own business and keeping an eye on my own undesirable habits and actions. I am merely telling you the law regarding the matter, and you may do the rest.

If you wish to choke out these habits, there are two ways open to you. First, whenever you find yourself indulging in a negative thought or feeling, take right hold of it and say to it firmly, and vigorously, "Get out!" It won't like this at first, and will bridle up, curve its back and snarl like an offended cat. But never mind - just say, "Scat" to it. The next time it will not be so confident and aggressive - it will have manifested a little of the fear-habit.

Each time you repress and choke out a tendency of this kind, the weaker it will become, and the stronger will your will be. Professor James says: "Refuse to express a passion, and it dies. Count ten before venting your anger, and its occasion seems ridiculous. Whistling to keep up courage is no mere figure of speech. On the other hand, sit all day in a moping posture, sigh, and reply to everything with a dismal voice, and your melancholy lingers.

There is no more valuable precept in moral education than this, as all who have experience know: if we wish to conquer emotional tendencies in ourselves, we must assiduously, and in the first instance, cold-bloodedly, go through the outward movements of those contrary dispositions we prefer to cultivate. Smooth the brow, brighten the eye, contract the dorsal rather than the ventral aspect of the frame, and speak in a major key, pass the genial compliment, and your heart must be frigid indeed if it does not gradually thaw.

CHAPTER 11 SUMMARY - The Psychology of Emotion

Emotions are based on habit. We may repress, increase, develop, and choose one's emotions, just as one may regulate habits of action and lines of thought. Each time you repress and choke out tendency of this kind, the weaker it will become, and the stronger will your "will" be. If we wish to conquer emotional tendencies in ourselves, AS SOON AS WE NOTICE THEM, we must rigorously, cold-bloodedly, instill the personality traits we want to become a habit.

Key Points:

- Emotions and actions are largely dependent upon habit.
- Worry grows with repetition to become a consistent habit.
- Once you give way to an undesirable emotion, it's easy to repeat.
- Each time you repress and choke out a negative tendency, the weaker it will become, and the stronger will your will be.
- Refuse to express a passion and it dies.

EXERCISE 11

1.   In left column below create a list of things that irritate you about others and/or yourself.

2.   Read each carefully and notice how you now react to this irritation?

3.   In right column below write how down a possible reaction in the future that could make a difference?

IRRITANTS   NEW REACTION

1. *Ex: Inconsiderate people anger me*   1. *I'm grateful that I know better*

2.   2.

3.   3.

4.   4.

5.   5.

6.   6.

7   7.

CHAPTER TWELVE

Developing New Brain Cells

I have spoken of the plan of getting rid of undesirable states of feeling by driving them out. But a far better way is to cultivate the feeling or emotion directly opposed to the one you wish to eradicate. We are very apt to regard ourselves as the creatures of our emotions and feelings, and to fancy that these feelings and emotions are "we." But such is far from being the truth.

It is true that the majority of the race are slaves of their emotions and feelings, and are governed by them to a great degree. They think that feelings are things that rule one and from which one cannot free himself, and so they cease to rebel. They yield to the feeling without question, although they may know that the emotion or mental trait is calculated to injure them, and to bring unhappiness and failure instead of happiness and success. They say, "We are made that way," and let it go at that.

The new Psychology is teaching the people better things. It tells them that they are masters of their emotions and feelings, instead of being their slaves. It tells them that brain-cells may be developed that will manifest along desirable lines, and that the old brain-cells that have been manifesting so unpleasantly may be placed on the retired list, and allowed to atrophy from want of use.

People may make themselves over, and change their entire natures. This is not mere idle theory, but is a working fact which has been demonstrated by thousands of people, and which is coming more and more before the attention of the race. No matter what theory of mind we entertain, we must admit that the brain is the organ and instrument of the mind, in our present state of existence, at least, and that the brain must be considered in this matter.

The brain is like a wonderful musical instrument, having millions of keys, upon which we may play innumerable combinations of sounds. We come into the world with certain tendencies, temperaments, and pre-dispositions. We may account for these tendencies by heredity, or we may account for them upon theories of pre-existence, but the facts remain the same.

Certain keys seem to respond to our touch more easily than others. Certain notes seem to sound forth as the current of circumstances sweeps over the strings. And certain other notes are less easily vibrated. But we find that if we but make an effort of the will to restrain the utterance of some of these easily sounded strings, they will grow more difficult to sound, and less liable to be stirred by the passing breeze. And if we will pay attention to some of the other strings that have not been giving forth a clear tone, we will soon get them in good working order; their notes will chime forth clear and vibrant, and will drown the less pleasant sounds.

We have millions of unused brain-cells awaiting our cultivation. We are using but a few of them, and some of these we are working to death. We are able to give some of these cells a rest, by using other cells. The brain may be trained and cultivated in a manner incredible to one who has not looked into the subject. Mental attitudes may be acquired and cultivated, changed and discarded, at will.

There is no longer any excuse for people manifesting unpleasant and harmful mental states. We have the remedy in our own hands. We acquire habits of thought, feeling, and action, repeated use. We may be born with a tendency in a certain direction, or we may acquire tendencies by suggestions from other; such as the examples of those around us, suggestions from reading, listening to teachers.

We are a bundle of mental habits. Each time we indulge in an undesirable thought or habit, the easier does it become for us to repeat that thought or action. Mental scientists are in the habit of speaking of desirable thoughts or mental attitudes as "positive," and of the undesirable ones as "negative." There is a good reason for this.

The mind instinctively recognizes certain things as good for the individual to which it belongs, and it clears the path for such thoughts, and interposes the least resistance to them. They have a much greater effect than an undesirable thought possesses, and one positive thought will counteract a number of negative thoughts.

The best way to overcome undesirable or negative thoughts and feelings is to cultivate the positive ones. The positive thought is the strongest plant, and will in time starve out the negative one by withdrawing from it the nourishment necessary for its existence. Of course the negative thought will set up a vigorous resistance at first, for it is a fight for life with it. In the slang words of the time, it "sees its finish" if the positive thought is allowed to grow and develop; and, consequently it makes things unpleasant for the individual until he has started well into the work of starving it out.

Brain cells do not like to be laid on the shelf any more than does any other form of living energy, and they rebel and struggle until they become too weak to do so. The best way is to pay as little attention as possible to these weeds of the mind, but put in as much time as possible watering, caring for and attending to the new and beautiful plants in the garden of the mind.

For instance, if you are apt to hate people, you can best overcome the negative thought by cultivating Love in its place. Think Love, and act it out, as often as possible. Cultivate thoughts of kindness, and act as kindly as you can to everyone with whom you come in contact. You will have trouble at the start, but gradually Love will master Hate, and the latter will begin to droop and wither.

If you have a tendency toward the "blues" cultivate a smile, and a cheerful view of things. Insist upon your mouth wearing upturned corners, and make an effort of the will to look upon the bright side of things. The "blue-devils" will set up a fight, of course, but pay no attention to them - just go on cultivating optimism and cheerfulness. Let "Bright, Cheerful and Happy" be your watchword, and try to live it out.

These recipes may seem very old and timeworn, but they are psychological truths and may be used by you to advantage. If you once comprehend the nature of the thing, the affirmations and autosuggestions of the several schools may be understood and taken advantage of. You may make yourself energetic instead of slothful, active instead of lazy, by this method. It is all a matter of practice and steady work.

New Thought people often have much to say about "holding the thought;" and, indeed, it is necessary to "hold the thought" in order to accomplish results. But something more is needed. You must "act out" the thought until it becomes a fixed habit with you. Thoughts take form in action; and in turn actions influence thought. So by "acting out" certain lines of thought, the actions react upon the mind, and increase the development of the part of the mind having close relation to the act.

Each time the mind entertains a thought, the easier becomes the resulting action - and each time an act is performed, the easier becomes the corresponding thought. So you see the thing works both ways - action and reaction. If you feel cheerful and happy, it is very natural for you to laugh. And if you will laugh a little, you will begin to feel bright and cheerful. Do you see what I am trying to get at?

Here it is, in a nutshell: if you wish to cultivate a certain habit of action, begin by cultivating the mental attitude corresponding to it. And as a means of cultivating that mental attitude, start in to "act-out " or go through, the motions of the act corresponding to the thought. Now, see if you cannot apply this rule. Take up something that you really feel should be done, but which you do not feel like doing. Cultivate the thought leading up to it - say to yourself: "I like to do so and so," and then go through the motions (cheerfully, remember!) and act out the thought that you like to do the thing.

Take an interest in the doing - study out the best way to do it - put brains into it - take a pride in it - and you will find yourself doing the thing with a considerable amount of pleasure and interest - you will have cultivated a new habit. If you prefer trying it on some mental trait of which you wish to be rid, it will work the same way. Start in to cultivate the opposite trait, and think it out and act it out for all you are worth. Then watch the change that will come over you.

Don't be discouraged at the resistance you will encounter at first, but sing gaily: "I Can and I Will," and get to work in earnest. The important thing in this work is to keep cheerful and interested. If you manage to do this, the rest will be easy.

CHAPTER 12 SUMMARY – Developing New Brain Cells

The brain may be trained and cultivated in a manner incredible to one who has not looked into the subject. Mental attitudes may be acquired and cultivated, changed and discarded, at will. We acquire habits of thought, feeling and action through repeated use. You must "act out" the thought until it becomes a fixed habit with you. Thoughts take form in action, and in turn actions influence thought. Each time the mind entertains a thought, the easier becomes the resulting action. Each time an act is performed, the easier becomes the corresponding thought.

Key Points:

- The brain may be trained and cultivated.
- You can master your emotions and feelings through habit.
- We acquire habits thru repeated use.
- Positive thoughts are stronger and can kill the negative ones but not without a fight.
- Thoughts take form in action, and in turn actions influence thought.
- Each time the mind entertains a thought, the easier becomes the resulting action.

EXERCISE 12

1. Do an act of kindness every day and keep a log.
2. Try doing it for 21 days straight. Continue list below.

1. *Example: I took my neighbors trash can from the curb.*

2.

3.

4.

5.

6.

7.

8.

9.

10.

CHAPTER THIRTEEN

The Attractive Power – Desire Force

WE have discussed the necessity of getting rid of fear, that your desire may have full strength with which to work. Supposing that you have mastered this part of the task, or at least started on the road to mastery, I will now call your attention to another important branch of the subject. I allude to the subject of mental leaks.

No, I don't mean the leakage arising from your failure to keep your own secrets - that is also important, but forms another story. The leakage I am now referring to is that occasioned by the habit of having the attention attracted to and distracted by every passing fancy.

In order to attain a thing it is necessary that the mind should fall in love with it, and be conscious of its existence, almost to the exclusion of everything else. You must get in love with the thing you wish to attain, just as much as you would if you were to meet the girl or man you wished to marry.

I do not mean that you should become a monomaniac upon the subject, and should lose all interest in everything else in the world - that won't do, for the mind must have recreation and change. But, I do mean that you must be so "set" upon the desired thing that all else will seem of secondary importance.

A man in love may be pleasant to everyone else, and may go through the duties and pleasures of life with good spirit, but underneath it all he is humming to himself "Just One Girl;" and every one of his actions is bent toward getting that girl, and making a comfortable home for her. Do you see what I mean?

You must get in love with the thing you want, and you must get in love with it in earnest - none of this latter-day flirting, "on-today and off-tomorrow" sort of love, but the good old-fashioned kind, that used to make it impossible for a young man to get to sleep unless he took a walk around his best girl's house, just to be sure it was still there. That's the real kind! And the man or woman in search of success must make of that desired thing his ruling passion - he must keep his mind on the main chance.

Success is jealous - that's why we speak of her as feminine. She demands a man's whole affection, and if he begins flirting with other fair charmers, she soon turns her back upon him. If a man allows his strong interest in the main chance to be sidetracked, he will be the loser. Mental Force operates best when it is concentrated.

You must give to the desired thing your best and most earnest thought. Just as the man who is thoroughly in love will think out plans and schemes whereby he may please the fair one, so will the man who is in love with his work or business give it his best thought, and the result will be that a hundred and one plans will come into his field of consciousness, many of which are very important.

The mind works on the subconscious plane, remember, and almost always along the lines of the ruling passion or desire. It will fix up things, and patch together plans and schemes, and when you need them the most it will pop them into your consciousness, and you will feel like hurrahing, just as if you had received some valuable aid from outside.

But if you scatter your thought-force, the subconscious mind will not know just how to please you, and the result is that you are apt to be put off from this source of aid and assistance. Beside this, you will miss the powerful result of concentrated thought in the conscious working out of the details of your plans.

And then again the man whose mind is full of a dozen interests fails to exert the attracting power that is manifested by the man of the one ruling passion, and he fails to draw to him persons, things, and results that will aid in the working out of his plans, and will also fail to place himself in the current of attraction whereby he is brought into contact with those who will be glad to help him because of harmonious interests.

I have noticed, in my own affairs, that when I would allow myself to be side-tracked by anything outside of my regular line of work, it would be only a short time before my receipts dropped off, and my business showed signs of a lack of vitality. Now, many may say that this was because I left undone some things that I would have done if my mind had been centered on the business. This is true; but I have noticed like results in cases where there was nothing to be done - cases in which the seed was sown, and the crop was awaited. And in just such cases, as soon as I directed my thought to the matter the seed began to sprout.

I do not mean that I had to send out great mental waves with the idea of affecting people - not a bit of it. I simply began to realize what a good thing I had, and how much people wanted it, and how glad they would be to know of it and all that sort of thing, and lo! My thought seemed to vitalize the work, and the seed began to sprout. This is no mere fancy, for I have experienced it on several occasions; I have spoken to many others on the subject, and I find that our experiences tally perfectly. So don't get into the habit of permitting these mental leaks.

Keep your Desire fresh and active, and let it get in its work without interference from conflicting desires. Keep in love with the thing you wish to attain - feed your fancy with it - see it as accomplished already, but don't lose your interest. Keep your eye on the main chance, and keep your one ruling passion strong and vigorous. Don't be a mental polygamist - one mental love is all that a man needs - that is, one at a time.

Some scientists have claimed that something that might as well be called "Love" is at the bottom of the whole of life. They claim that the love of the plant for water causes it to send forth its roots until the loved thing is found. They say that the love of the flower for the sun causes it to grow away from the dark places, so that it may receive the light. The so-called "chemical affinities" are really a form of love. And Desire is a manifestation of this Universal Life Love. So I am not using a mere figure of speech when I tell you that you must love the thing you wish to attain.

Nothing but intense love will enable you to surmount the many obstacles placed in your path. Nothing but that love will enable you to bear the burdens of the task. The more Desire you have for a thing, the more you Love it; and the more you Love it, the greater will be the attractive force exerted toward its attainment - both within yourself, and outside of you. So love but one thing at a time.

CHAPTER 13 SUMMARY – The Attractive Power – Desire Force

Mental force operates best when it is concentrated. Keep your Desire fresh and active, and let it get in its work without interference from conflicting desires. A mental leak is the habit of having the attention attracted to and distracted by every passing fancy. Mental force operates best when it's concentrated. Give your best and most earnest thought to what you desire. Scattered thought force results in failure. One strong and vigorous mental love at a time is all you need.

Key Points:

- In order to attain a thing it is necessary that the mind should fall in love with it, and be conscious of its existence, almost to the exclusion of everything else.
- Mental force operates best when it is concentrated.
- Keep your Desire fresh and active, and let it get in its work without interference from conflicting desires.
- The mind works on the subconscious plane along the lines of ruling passion.
- The man with a dozen interests on his mind is scattered and will fail.
- Desire is a manifestation of Universal Life Love.
- You must keep your one ruling passion strong and vigorous.
- Nothing but intense love will enable you to surmount the many obstacles placed in your path.

EXERCISE 13

1. In your journal, write out what it is that you desire to manifest.

2. In a paragraph or two write out how it looks, feels, smells, tastes and the way it sounds. Write out every aspect of it.

3. Read this over, close your eyes and image what it looks like.

4. Continue this as a daily practice. Note any "surprises" in your journal.

Example:

I want to take my whole family on a cruise. We will be laughing, happy and completely relaxed. I can feel the breeze on my skin and the salty smell of the sea. We are at a family dinner where the seafood dinner is wonderfully delicious and everyone is acknowledging me for putting this together and paying for everything. My mother is smiling and very happy to be with all of her sons, daughters, grandkids and great-grandkids. We plan excursions together and everyone is floored when I give them shopping money so they can buy presents to take back. We are so happy and in love with each other and everything comes together flawlessly.

CHAPTER FOURTEEN

The Great Dynamic Forces

YOU have noticed the difference between the successful and strong men in any walk of life, and the unsuccessful weak men around them. You are conscious of the widely differing characteristics of the two classes, but somehow find it difficult to express just in what the difference lies. Let us take a look at the matter. Burton said:

"The longer I live, the more certain I am that the great difference between men, the feeble and the powerful, the great and the insignificant, is energy and invincible determination - a purpose once fixed and then Death or Victory. That quality will do anything that can be done in this world - and no talents, no circumstances, no opportunities will make a two-legged creature a man without it."

I do not see how the idea could be more clearly expressed than Burton has spoken. He has put his finger right in the center of the subject – his eye has seen into the heart of it. Energy and invincible determination - these two things will sweep away mighty barriers, and will surmount the greatest obstacles. And yet they must be used together.

Energy without determination will go to waste. Lots of men have plenty of energy - they are full to overflowing with it; and yet they lack concentration - they lack the concentrated force that enables them to bring their power to bear upon the right spot. Energy is not nearly so rare a thing as many imagine it to be.

I can look around me at any time, and pick out a number of people I know who are full of energy - many of them are energy plus — and yet, somehow, they do not seem to make any headway. They are wasting their energy all the time. Now they are fooling with this thing - now meddling with that. They will take up some trifling thing of no real interest or importance, and waste enough energy and nervous force to carry them through a hard day's work, and yet when they are through, nothing has been accomplished.

Others who have plenty of energy, fail to direct it by the power of the Will toward the desired end. "Invincible determination" - those are the words. Do they not thrill you with their power? If you have something to do, get to work and do it. Marshal your energy, and then guide and direct it by your Will - bestow upon it that "invincible determination" and you will do the thing.

Everyone has within him a giant will, but the majority of us are too lazy to use it. We cannot get ourselves nerved up to the point at which we can say, truthfully: "I Will. If we can but pluck up our courage to that point, and will then pin it in place so that it will not slip back, we will be able to call into play that wonderful power - the Human Will. Man, as a rule, has but the faintest conception of the power of the Will, but those who have studied along the occult teachings, know that the Will is one of the great dynamic forces of the universe, and if harnessed and directed properly it is capable of accomplishing almost miraculous things.

"Energy and Invincible Determination: -- aren't they magnificent words? Commit them to memory - press them like a die into the wax of your mind, and they will be a constant inspiration to you in hours of need. If you can get these words to vibrating in your being, you will be a giant among pygmies. Say these words over and over again, and see how you are filled with new life - see how your blood will circulate - how your nerves will tingle.

Make these words a part of yourself, and then go forth anew to the battle of life, encouraged and strengthened. Put them into practice. "Energy and Invincible Determination" - let that be your motto in your work-a-day life, and you will be one of those rare men who are able to "do things."

 Many persons are deterred from doing their best by the fact that they underrate themselves by comparison with the successful ones of life, or rather, overrate the successful ones by comparison with themselves. One of the curious things noticed by those who are brought in contact with the people who have "arrived" is the fact that these successful people are not extraordinary after all.

You meet with some great writer, and you are disappointed to find him very ordinary indeed. He does not converse brilliantly, and, in fact, you know a score of everyday people who seem far more brilliant than this man who dazzles you by his brightness in his books. You meet some great statesman, and he does not seem nearly as wise as lots of old fellows in your own village, who waste their wisdom upon the desert air. You meet some great captain of industry, and he does not give you the impression of the shrewdness so marked in some little bargain-driving trader in your own town. How is this, anyway? Are the reputations of these people fictitious, or what is the trouble?

The trouble is this: you have imagined these people to be made of superior metal, and are disappointed to find them made of the same stuff as yourself and those about you. But, you ask, wherein does their greatness of achievement lie? Chiefly in this: Belief in themselves and in their inherent power, in their faculty to concentrate on the work in hand, when they are working, and in their ability to prevent leaks of power when they are not working.

They believe in themselves, and make every effort count. Your village wise man spills his wisdom on every corner, and talks to a lot of fools; when if he really were wise he would save up his wisdom and place it where it would do some work.

The brilliant writer does not waste his wit upon every corner; in fact, he shuts the drawer in which he contains his wit, and opens it only when he is ready to concentrate and get down to business. The captain of industry has no desire to impress you with his shrewdness and "smartness. He never did, even when he was young. While his companions were talking and boasting, and "blowing," this future successful financier was "sawin' wood and sayin' nuthin'."

The great people of the world - that is, those who have "arrived" - are not very different from you, or me, or the rest of us - all of us are about the same at the base. You have only to meet them to see how very "ordinary" they are, after all. But, don't forget the fact that they know how to use the material that is in them; while the rest of the crowd does not, and, in fact, even doubts whether the true stuff is there.

The man or woman who "gets there", usually starts out by realizing that he or she is not so very different, after all, from the successful people that they hear so much about. This gives them confidence, and the result is they find out that they are able to "do things." Then they learn to keep their mouths closed, and to avoid wasting and dissipating their energy. They store up energy, and concentrate it upon the task at hand; while their companions are scattering their energies in every direction, trying to show off and let people know how smart they are.

The man or woman who "gets there," prefers to wait for the applause that follows deed accomplished, and cares very little for the praise that attends promises of what we expect to do "some day," or an exhibition of "smartness" without works.

One of the reasons that people who are thrown in with successful men often manifest success themselves, is that they are able to watch the successful man and sort of "catch the trick" of his greatness. They see that he is an everyday sort of man, but that he thoroughly believes in himself, and also that he does not waste energy, but reserves all his force for the actual tasks before him.

And, profiting by example, they start to work and put the lesson into practice in their own lives. Now what is the moral of this talk? Simply this: Don't undervalue yourself, or overvalue others. Realize that you are made of good stuff, and that locked within your mind are many good things. Then get to work and unfold those good things, and make something out of that good stuff.

Do this by attention to the things before you, and by giving to each the best that is in you, knowing that plenty of more good things are in you ready for the fresh tasks that will come. Put the best of yourself into the undertaking on hand, and do not cheat the present task in favor of some future one. Your supply is inexhaustible. And don't waste your good stuff on the crowd of gapers, watchers and critics who are standing around watching you work. Save your good stuff for your job, and don't be in too much of a hurry for applause.

Save up your good thoughts for "copy" if you are a writer; save up your bright schemes for actual practice, if you are a businessman; save up your wisdom for occasion, if you are a statesman; and, in each case, avoid the desire to scatter your pears before - well, before the gaping crowd that wants to be entertained by a "free show." Nothing very "high" about this teaching, perhaps, but it is what many of you need very much. Stop fooling, and get down to business. Stop wasting good raw material, and start to work making something worthwhile.

CHAPTER 14 SUMMARY – The Great Dynamic Forces

The difference between successful, strong men in any walk and unsuccessful weak men around them is energy and invincible determination it's not just an action – it is determination. The majority of us are too lazy to use our Will. It is one of the great dynamic forces of the universe, and if harnessed and directed properly it is capable of accomplishing almost miraculous things. Many persons are deterred from doing their best by the fact that they underrate themselves by comparison with the successful ones of life, or rather, overrate the successful ones by comparison with themselves. Successful people are not extraordinary after all. Their greatness of achievement lie in the belief in themselves and in their inherent power. Don't undervalue yourself, or overvalue others. Realize that you are made of good stuff, and that locked within your mind are many good things.

Key Points:

- Energy and Invincible Determination must be used together.
- Focus your energy, then guide and direct it by using your Will – treat it with "Invincible Determination" and you will "do the thing".
- Will is one of the great dynamic forces of the universe, and if harnessed and directed properly it is capable of accomplishing almost miraculous things.
- Believe in yourself and your inherent power.
- Store up energy and concentrate it upon the task at hand.
- Don't waste energy showing off for others, save your good stuff for your job.
- Keep yourself in one position. Aim your mind in one place.

EXERCISE 14

1. Create and write out a BOLD STATEMENT OF PASSION that gets you excited.

2. In your journal write down what that would look like once fulfilled.

3. Create and write out what you think a plan of action around accomplishing that which you desire would entail.

4. Remember that life is a game and can be flexible.

Example: I will earn 2x more income this year than last year.

My plan is to create at least 3 additional sources of income that are fun and enjoyable.

CHAPTER FIFTEEN

Claiming Your Own

In a recent conversation, I was telling a woman to pluck up courage and to reach out for a certain good thing for which she had been longing for many years, and which, at last, appeared to be in sight. I told her that it looked as if her desire was about to be gratified - that the Law of Attraction was bringing it to her.

She lacked faith, and kept on repeating, "Oh! It's too good to be true - it's too good for me! She had not emerged from the worm-of-the-dust stage, and although she was in sight of the Promised Land she refused to enter it because it "was too good for her." l think I succeeded in putting sufficient "ginger" into her to enable her to claim her own, for the last reports indicate that she is taking possession.

But that is not what I wish to tell you. I want to call your attention to the fact that nothing is too good for YOU - no matter how great the thing may be - no matter how undeserving you may seem to be. You are entitled to the best there is, for it is your direct inheritance. So don't be afraid to ask - demand - and take.

The good things of the world are not the portion of any favored sons. They belong to all, but they come only to those who are wise enough to recognize that the good things are theirs by right, and who are sufficiently courageous to reach out for them. Many good things are lost for want of the asking. Many splendid things are lost to you because of your feeling that you are unworthy of them.

Many great things are lost to you because you lack the confidence and courage to demand and take possession of them. "None but the brave deserves the fair," says the old adage, and the rule is true in all lines of human effort.

If you keep on repeating that you are unworthy of the good thing - that it is too good for you - the Law will be apt to take you at your word and believe what you say. That's a peculiar thing about the Law - it believes - what you say - it takes you in earnest. So beware what you say to it, for it will be apt to give credence.

Say to it that you are worthy of the best there is, and that there is nothing too good for you, and you will be likely to have the Law take you in earnest, and say, "I guess he is right; I'm going to give him the whole bakeshop if he wants it - he knows his rights, and what's the use of trying to deny it to him?" But if you say, "Oh, it's too good for me! The Law will probably say, "Well, I wouldn't wonder but that that is so. Surely he ought to know, and it isn't for me to contradict him." And so it goes.

Why should anything be too good for you? Did you ever stop to think just what you are? You are a manifestation of the Whole Thing, and have a perfect right to all there is. Or, if you prefer it this way, you are a child of the Infinite, and are heir to it all. You are telling the truth in either statement, or both. At any rate, no matter for what you ask, you are merely demanding your own. And the more in earnest you are about demanding it – the more confident you are of receiving it - the more will you use in reaching out for it – the surer you will be to obtain it.

Strong desire - confident expectation - courage in action - these things bring to you your own. But before you put these forces into effect, you must awaken to a realization that you are merely asking for your own, and not for something to which you have no right or claim. So long as there exists in your mind the last sneaking bit of doubt as to your right to the things you want, you will be setting up a resistance to the operation of the Law. You may demand as vigorously as you please, but you will lack the courage to act, if you have a lingering doubt of your right to the thing you want.

If you persist in regarding the desired thing as if it belonged to another, instead of to yourself, you will be placing yourself in the position of the covetous or envious man, or even in the position of a tempted thief. In such a case your mind will revolt at proceeding with the work, for it instinctively will recoil from the idea of taking what is not your own - the mind is honest.

But when your realize that the best the Universe holds belongs to you as a Divine Heir, and that there is enough for all without your robbing anyone else; then the friction is removed, and the barrier broken down, and the Law proceeds to do its work. I do not believe in this "humble" business. This meek and lowly attitude does not appeal to me - there is no sense in it, at all.

The idea of making a virtue of such things, when Man is the heir of the Universe, and is entitled to whatever he needs for his growth, happiness and satisfaction! I do not mean that one should assume a blustering and domineering attitude of mind - that is also absurd, for true strength does not so exhibit itself. The blusterer is a self-confessed weakling - he blusters to disguise his weakness.

The truly strong man is calm, self-contained, and carries with him a consciousness of strength which renders unnecessary the bluster and fuss of assumed strength. But get away from this hypnotism of "humility" - this "meek and lowly" attitude of mind. Remember the horrible example of Uriah Heep, and beware of imitating him. Throw back you head, and look the world square in the face. There's nothing to be afraid of - the world is apt to be as much afraid of you, as you are of it, anyway. Be a man, or woman, and not a crawling thing.

And this applies to your mental attitude, as well as to your outward demeanor. Stop this crawling in your mind. See yourself as standing erect and facing life without fear, and you will gradually grow into your ideal. There is nothing that is too good for you - not a thing. The best there is, is not beginning to be good enough for you; for there are still better things ahead. The best gift that the world has to offer is a mere bauble compared to the great things in the Cosmos that await your coming of age. So don't be afraid to reach out for these playthings of life - these baubles of this plane of consciousness. Reach out for them - grab a whole fistful - play with them until you are tired; that's what they are made for, anyway. They are made for our express use - not to look at, but to be played with, if you desire.

Help yourself - there's a whole shop-full of these toys awaiting your desire, demand and taking. Don't be bashful! Don't let me hear any more of this silly talk about things being too good for you. Pshaw! You have been like the Emperor's little son thinking that the tin soldiers and toy drum were far too good for him, and refusing to reach out for them.

But you don't find this trouble with children as a rule. They instinctively recognize that nothing is too good for them. They want all that is in sight to play with, and they seem to feel that the things are theirs by right. And that is the condition of mind that we seekers after the Divine Adventure must cultivate. Unless we become as little children we cannot enter the Kingdom of Heaven.

The things we see around us are the playthings of the Kindergarten of God, playthings which we use in our game-tasks. Help yourself to them - ask for them without bashfulness demand as many as you can make use of - they are yours. And if you don't see just what you want, ask for it - there's a big reserve stock on the shelves, and in the closets. Play, play, play, to your heart's content.

Learn to weave mats - to build houses with the blocks - to stitch outlines on the squares - play the game through, and play it well. And demand all the proper materials for the play - don't be bashful - there's enough to go round. But - remember this! While all this be true, the best things are still only game-things - toys, blocks, mats, cubes, and all the rest. Useful, most useful for the learning of the lessons - pleasant, most pleasant with which to play - and desirable, most desirable, for these purposes.

Get all the fun and profit out of the use of things that is possible. Throw yourself heartily into the game, and play it out - it is Good. But, here's the thing to remember - never lose sight of the fact that these good things are but playthings - part of the game - and you must be perfectly willing to lay them aside when the time comes to pass into the next class, and not cry and mourn because you must leave your playthings behind you.

Do not allow yourself to become unduly attached to them – they are for your use and pleasure, but are not a part of you - not essential to your happiness in the next stage. Despise them not because of their lack of Reality - they are great things relatively, and you may as well have all the fun out of them that you can - don't be a spiritual prig, standing aside and refusing to join in the game.

But do not tie yourself to them - they are good to use and play with, but not good enough to use you and to make you a plaything. Don't let the toys turn the tables on you. This is the difference between the Master of Circumstances and the Slave of Circumstances. The Slave thinks that these playthings are real, and that he is not good enough to have them. He gets only a few toys, because he is afraid to ask for more, and he misses most of the fun. And then, considering the toys to be real, and not realizing that there are plenty more where these came from, he attaches himself to the little trinkets that have come his way, and allows himself to be made a slave of them. He is afraid that they may be taken away from him and he is afraid to toddle across the floor and help himself to the others.

The Master knows that all are his for the asking. He demands that which he needs from day to day, and does not worry about overloading himself; for he knows that there are "lots more," and that he cannot be cheated out of them. He plays, and plays well, and has a good time in the play - and he learns his Kindergarten lessons in the playing. But he does not become too much attached to his toys.

He is willing to fling away the worn-out toys, and reach out for a new one. And when he is called into the next room for promotion, he drops on the floor the worn-out toys of the day, and with glistening eyes and confident attitude of mind, marches into the next room - into the Great Unknown - with a smile on his face. He is not afraid, for he hears the voice of the Teacher, and knows that she is there waiting for him - in that Great Next Room.

CHAPTER 15 SUMMARY - Claiming Your Own

The good life is available to everyone, not just a select few. But it can only come to you if you know it's yours and are not afraid to reach for them. Many good things are lost because you didn't ask. You must cultivate strong desire, confident expectation and use courage in action. Courage is being scared and acting anyway. Strong desire, confident expectation, courage in action bring you what you desire. It's already yours, but if you have any sneaking doubt, you can demand but you will not have the courage to act. The mind is honest. It will resist because it thinks it's stealing something that is not your own. Beware of what you say. Once you have created that which you desire, do not become attached. You must be willing to let go of the old, and allow the new to come in.

Key Points:

- You are a child of the Infinite, and are heir to it all.
- STRONG DESIRE – CONFIDENT EXPECTATION – COURAGE IN ACTION – these things bring to you your own.
- Doing this work will manifest for you.
- You are entitled to all you desire.
- Children instinctively know that nothing is too good for them.
- You must cultivate the mind of a child.
- Help yourself to the play things in the kindergarten of God.
- Know that you are entitled to all but do not develop attachment.
- Don't worry – always remember there is lots more.

EXERCISE 15

1. Strong Desire – Write out what you strongly desire.

2. Confident Expectation – Write out what you expect this to look like while waiting for your desire to manifest.

3. Courage in Action – Write out what you think it looks like to be courageous in action.

Example: I desire to have more money than I could ever spend this lifetime.

I will relax, ask the Universe for guidance then listen to my inner voice and create something that can be sold for lots and lots of money.

It would be courageous for me to ask someone to help me to develop some of the ideas that come into my mind.

CHAPTER SIXTEEN

Law, Not Chance

SOME time ago I was talking to a man about the Attractive Power of Thought. He said that he did not believe that Thought could attract anything to him, and that it was all a matter of luck. He had found, he said, that ill luck relentlessly pursued him, and that everything he touched went wrong. It always had, and always would, and he had grown to expect it. When he undertook a new thing he knew beforehand that it would go wrong and that no good would come of it. Oh, no! There wasn't anything in the theory of Attractive Thought, so far as he could see; it was all a matter of luck!

This man failed to see that by his own confession he was giving a most convincing argument in favor of the Law of Attraction. He was testifying that he was always expecting things to go wrong, and that they always came about as he expected. He was a magnificent illustration of the Law of Attraction - but he didn't know it, and no argument seemed to make the matter clear to him. He was "up against it," and there was no way out of it - he always expected the ill luck and every occurrence proved that he was right, and that the Mental Science position was all nonsense.

There are many people who seem to think that the only way in which the Law of Attraction operates is when one wishes hard, strong and steady. They do not seem to realize that a strong belief is as efficacious as a strong wish.

The successful man believes in himself and his ultimate success, and, paying no attention to little setbacks, stumbles, tumbles and slips, presses on eagerly to the goal, believing all the time that he will get there. His views and aims may alter as he progresses, and he may change his plans or have them changed for him, but all the time he knows in his heart that he will eventually "get there."

He is not steadily wishing he may get there - he simply feels and believes it, and thereby sets to operation the strongest forces known in the world of thought.

The man who just as steadily believes he is going to fail will invariably fail. How could he help it? There is no special miracle about it. Everything he does, thinks, and says is tinctured with the thought of failure. Other people catch his spirit, and fail to trust him or his ability, which occurrences he in turn sets down as but other exhibitions of his ill luck, instead of ascribing them to his belief and expectation of failure.

He is suggesting failure to himself all the time, and he invariably takes on the effect of the autosuggestion. Then, again, he by his negative thoughts shuts up that portion of his mind from which should come the ideas and plans conducive to success and which do come to the man who is expecting success because he believes in it.

A state of discouragement is not the one in which bright ideas come to us. It is only when we are enthused and hopeful that our minds work out the bright ideas which we may turn to account. Men instinctively feel the atmosphere of failure hovering around certain of their fellows, and on the other hand recognize something about others which leads them to say, when they hear of a temporary mishap befalling such a one: "Oh, he'll come out all right somehow - you can't down him." It is the atmosphere caused by the prevailing Mental Attitude.

Clear up your Mental Atmosphere! There is no such thing as chance. Law maintains everywhere, and all that happens because of the operation of Law. You cannot name the simplest thing that ever occurred by chance - try it, and then run the thing down to a final analysis, and you will see it as the result of law.

It is as plain as mathematics. Plan and purpose; cause and effect. From the movements of worlds to the growth of the grain of mustard seed - all the result of Law. The fall of the stone down the mountainside is not chance - forces which had been in operation for centuries caused it. And back of that cause were other causes, and so on until the Causeless Cause is reached. And Life is not the result of chance - the Law is here, too.

The Law is in full operation whether you know it or not - whether you believe in it or not. You may be the ignorant object upon which the Law operates, and bring yourself all sorts of trouble because of your ignorance of or opposition to the Law. Or you may fall in with the operations to the Law - get into its current, as it were - and Life will seem a far different thing to you.

You cannot get outside of the Law, by refusing to have anything to do with it. You are at liberty to oppose it and produce all the friction you wish to - it doesn't' hurt the Law, and you may keep it up until you learn your lesson. The Law of Thought Attraction is one name for the law, or rather for one manifestation of it.

Again I say, your thoughts are real things. They go forth from you in all directions, combining with thoughts of like kind, opposing thoughts of a different character, forming combinations - going where they are attracted - flying away from thought centers opposing them.

And your mind attracts the thought of others, which have been sent out by them conscious or unconsciously. But it attracts only those thoughts which are in harmony with its own.

Like attracts like, and opposites repel opposites, in the world of thought. If you set your mind to the keynote of courage, confidence, strength and success, you attract to yourself thoughts of like nature; people of like nature; things that fit in the mental tune.

Your prevailing thought or mood determines that which is to be drawn toward you - picks out your mental bedfellow. You are today setting into motion thought currents which will in time attract toward you thoughts, people and conditions in harmony with the predominant note of your thought.

Your thought will mingle with that of others of like nature and mind, and you will be attracted toward each other, and will surely come together with a common purpose sooner or later, unless one or the other of you should change the current of his thoughts. Fall in with the operations of the law. Make it a part of yourself. Get into its currents. Maintain your poise. Set your mind to the keynote of Courage, Confidence and Success.

Get in touch with all the thoughts of that kind that are emanating every hour from hundreds of minds. Get the best that is to be had in the thought world. The best is there, so be satisfied with nothing less. Get into partnership with good minds. Get into the right vibrations. You must be tired of being tossed about by the operations of the Law - get into harmony with It.

CHAPTER 16 SUMMARY– Law, Not Chance

The Law of Attraction is a force that is always working. Some say that things are the way they are and if anything good happens it's just luck. Belief is a powerful tool. You are successful when you believe in yourself and your ultimate success, paying no attention to minor setbacks. If you think or say you will fail, most assuredly you will. You can only attract those thoughts that are in harmony with its own. Like attracts like, opposites repel opposites in the world of thought.

Key Points:

- So called "luck" as well as "misfortunes" is attracted by your words and thoughts.
- A strong belief is just as effective and a strong wish.
- You must believe in your ultimate success disregarding the setbacks.
- Your thoughts are real things that go out in all directions.
- FEEL and BELIEVE and you set in motion the strongest forces known in the world of thought.
- Be satisfied with nothing less than the best.
- Your prevailing thought or mood determines that which is to be drawn toward you.
- Get in harmony with the law and create what you desire.

EXERCISE 16

Write down 3 statements of something you desire and believe you can now have. State it as, "I now believe that I can…"

Make copies of these statements and put them in inconspicuous places to be read on occasion.

Example: I now believe that I can make more money than I ever have before.

Author's notes: Each week comments will be posted from participants who have been using the workbook at MyProspserityAdviser.com. Just look for Thought Vibrations Workbook and see what others are saying about their experience. These exercises were designed to put each chapter into your life on an experiential level.

Novella would love to hear from you at MyProsperityAdviser.com.

Novella Williams, an Empowerment coach and consultant for fifteen years, is very passionate about people understanding the power of their own words. She believes that the Universe hears what we say whether conscious or unconsciously and responds to our thoughts. With the right tools, simple steps to follow and easy quick exercises, people have the ability to turn a practice into a habit.

Raised in Detroit Michigan, Novella has devoted her life to discovering who she is and who others are beyond their limitations. She embraces and demonstrates this philosophy in her day to day life. Her life is filled with unique "every day" experiences in celebration of her efforts. She has walked arm in arm with Maya Angelou and visited the home of Winnie Mandela through what some would call "chance" or "coincidence". She calls it the "power of word". She believes that if people change their words, they can change their lives and ultimately their world.

Novella strongly supports and believes that when people come to realize this power, it will rid the world of racism and divisiveness, hunger and hatred and allow people to fall in love with the unique eloquence of individuality. Her life's mission is for all people to be joyfully self-expressed living together in cultural harmony. One of her practices and passions is hosting occasions for women to come together in camaraderie and sisterhood. She is also the Director of the non-profit organization, Healing Thru Arts where art is used as a means to heal the planet.

www.ingramcontent.com/pod-product-compliance
Lightning Source LLC
Chambersburg PA
CBHW061737020426
42331CB00006B/1268